Entrepreneurial Librarianship

Entrepreneurial Librarianship:

The Key to Effective Information Services Management

Guy St Clair

London • Melbourne • Munich • New Jersey

British Library Cataloguing in Publication Data
A catalogue record for this book is available from the British Library

Library of Congress Cataloging-in-Publication Data
A catalog record for this book is available from the Library of Congress

Published by Bowker-Saur,
Maypole House,
Maypole Road,
East Grinstead,
West Sussex RH19 1HU, UK
Tel: +44(0)1342 330100 Fax: +44(0)1342 330191
E-mail: lis@bowker-saur.co.uk
Internet Website: http://www.bowker-saur.co.uk/service

Bowker-Saur is part of REED REFERENCE PUBLISHING

ISBN 1-85739-014-8

Cover design by Juan Hayward
Typesetting by Florencetype Ltd, Stoodleigh, Devon
Printed on acid-free paper
Printed and bound in Great Britain by
Bell & Bain Ltd, Glasgow

The author

Guy St Clair is the president of SMR International, a management consulting, training and publishing company based in New York. The company's clients include major chemical, pharmaceutical and engineering firms, and information organizations connected with the federal government, medicine, the arts, professional associations and the academic community. SMR International is also known as the publisher of *InfoManage: The International Management Newsletter for the Information Services Executive* and *The One-Person Library: A Newsletter for Librarians and Management*. In London, the company is represented by TFPL Ltd, through which its services are offered to the European market. Guy St Clair is a past president of the Special Libraries Association (1991-1992) and he is an active member and participant in the Information Futures Institute. An alumnus of the University of Virginia (BA), with his graduate work at the University of Illinois (MSLS), Guy St Clair lives in New York City.

This book is dedicated to
Andrew Berner
. . . and to
Beth Duston,
because more than anyone else I know,
she understands the value
of entrepreneurial thinking
in the information environment

Introduction to the series

A broader management perspective for information services

For several years, decades it seems, librarians and other information services professionals have lamented the fact that there is not enough emphasis on management in their training. They learn their subjects, and librarians, especially, connect very early on in their training to the concepts of service and the organization of information. Management skills, however, are frequently neglected, or given minimal attention, and many information services professionals find themselves working in the corporate environment, research and technology organizations, government information units, or community/public administration organizations where management skills are needed. Much of what they need they get on the job; other approaches, such as continuing education programs, are utilized by those who have the initiative to recognize that they must do something to educate themselves to be managers. Some of it works and some of it does not.

Bowker-Saur's *Information Services Management Series*, for which I serve as Series Editor, seeks to address this need in the information services community. For this series (and indeed, since the entire field of information management is strongly predicted by many to be going in this direction), the concept of information services is being defined very broadly. The time has come, it seems to me, to recognize that the various constituent units of our society concerned with information have many of the same goals, objectives, and not surprisingly, many of the same concerns. The practice of management is one of these, and for our purposes, it does not matter if the reader of these books is employed as an information manager, information provider, information specialist, or indeed, as an information counsellor (as these information workers have been described by one of the leaders of business and industry). In fact, it does not matter whether the reader is employed in information technology, telecommunications, traditional librarianship, records management, corporate or organizational archives, the information brokerage field, publishing, consulting, or any of the myriad branches of information services (including service to the information community and the many vendors who make up that branch of the profession). These new titles on the management of information services have been chosen specifically for their value to all who are part of this community of information workers.

While much work is being done in these various disciplines, little of it concentrates on management, and that which is done generally concentrates on one or another of the specific subgroups of the field. This series seeks to unite management concepts throughout information services, and while some of the titles will be directed to a specific group, most will be broad-based and will attempt to address issues of concern to all information services employees. For example, this book deals with entrepreneurial librarianship, which would seem to be limited to the library profession, but in fact the book, I hope, offers information and guidance of use to anyone working in the information services field who is willing to incorporate entrepreneurial thinking into his or her work.

It will be pointed out, of course, that the practice of management in information services is addressed within the organizations or communities which employ information workers. This is true, and certainly in the corporate world (and, arguably, in the public and academic library communities as well), there are plenty of occasions for information services employees to participate in management training as provided in-house. There is nothing wrong with that approach, and in many organizations it works very well, but the training does not proceed from an information services point of view, thus forcing the information worker to adapt, as best he or she can, the management practices of the organization to the management practices needed for the best provision of information services. The titles to appear in the Bowker-Saur *Information Services Management Series* will enable the information worker to relate *information* management to *organizational* management, thus putting the information worker (especially the information executive) in a position of considerable strength in the organization or community where he or she is employed. By understanding management principles (admittedly, as frequently 'borrowed' from the general practice of management) and relating them to the way the information services unit is organized, the information services employee not only positions himself or herself for the better provision of information services, but the entire information services unit is positioned as a respectable participant in organizational or community operations.

This last point perhaps needs some elaboration, for it should be made clear that the books in the series are not intended exclusively for the corporate or specialized information services field. It is our intention to provide useful management criteria for all kinds of information services, including those connected to public, academic, or other publicly supported libraries.

Our basic thesis is that quality management leads to quality services, regardless of whether the information services activity is privately or publicly funded, whether it is connected with a private research institution or a public governmental agency, or indeed, whether it is a temporary information unit or whether it is part of a permanently funded and staffed operation. Writing for this series will be authors, who, I am sure, will challenge some of the usual barriers to effective management practices in this or that type of library or information services unit, and certainly there will be librarians, records managers, archivists and others who will be able to relate some of their management practices in such a way that CIOs and computer services managers will benefit from the telling. In other words, our attempt here is to clear away the usual preconceptions about management within the various branches of information services, to do away with the very concept of 'well-that-might-work-for-you-but-it-won't-work-for-me' kind of thinking. We can no longer afford to fight turf battles about whether or not management is 'appropriate' in one or another of the various subunits of information provision. What we must do, and what the *Information Services Management Series* expects to do, is to bring together the best of all of us, and to share our management expertise so that we all benefit.

Guy St Clair
Series Editor

Contents

Introduction

Embracing the entrepreneurial perspective

Every practice rests on theory, even if the practitioners themselves are unaware of it. Entrepreneurship rests on a theory of economy and society. The theory sees change as normal and indeed as healthy. And it sees the major task in society—and especially in the economy—as doing something different rather than doing better what is already being done. This is basically what [French economist] J.B. Say, two hundred years ago, meant when he coined the term *entrepreneur*. It was intended as a manifesto and as a declaration of dissent: the entrepreneur upsets and disorganizes. As Joseph Schumpeter formulated it, his task is 'creative destruction'.

(Drucker, 1985, p. 26)

Innovation depends on organized abandonment. When the French economist J.B. Say coined the word 'entrepreneur' 200 years ago, he meant it as a manifesto and a declaration of intent: the entrepreneur in his scheme was someone who upsets and disorganizes. To get at the new and better, you have to throw out the old, outworn, obsolete, no longer productive, as well as the mistakes, failure, and misdirection of effort of the past.

(Drucker, 1992, p. 340)

To introduce a book with not one but two quotations from the same source says as much about the author and his inspiration as it does about the subject the quotations embrace. Without apology, I heartily acknowledge the influence that Peter F. Drucker has had in the development of my thinking about this and many other subjects having to do with the management of information services. Drucker (and others, too, I am not reluctant to add) has long had much to say that transfers easily and appropriately into the field of information services, and when I look at how often Drucker and many of these other influential thinkers are quoted in the literature, I find myself in rather exalted company, for many of the leaders in information services turn to them for inspiration. These authors and teachers are much at work in our society today, showing us how we can use the concepts and theories of management in a great variety of fields in which management as a discipline was, for many generations, eschewed. We who are employed in information services are wise to turn to them for guidance as we seek to become better at what we do.

This book advocates that practitioners in library and information services embrace an entrepreneurial perspective for their work, so it only follows that the above quotations provide an appropriate point of reference. By and large, we in librarianship and information services are very satisfied with what we do. Our customers do not generally go away unhappy, although they may be less than satisfied when we have provided them with only part of the information they came to us to obtain. But even in those cases, because of the general 'warm' feeling that most lay people have about libraries and other information services operations, there is a general sense of tolerant acceptance. And for many practitioners in the field, that seems to be all right. It's almost as if we've fallen into the 'we're OK' trap, with 'OK' being the standard by which our services and our professional activities are judged. Excellence, that standard which so far surpasses 'OK' and which requires so much more work from us, is often left behind as being too much trouble to achieve.

But such an attitude won't work any more, because librarianship – as a part of the overall information services field – is starting to be judged by the same standards of quality, excellence and accountability that all other information services are judged by. Indeed, the requirement for accountability now pervades much of society (certainly the productive and service economics of society) and the entire information services field, including librarianship, must justify itself to those who have decision-making authority about the resources that support the existence of those services. When the judgment is made, if librarianship is found wanting it will be done away with.

So we have no choice but to assume an entrepreneurial stance and to look to do something different, for merely doing better what is already being done will leave us as a profession standing absolutely still. That is what this book is about. It is an attempt to look at entrepreneurial management and to come to some conclusions about how the entrepreneurial perspective can be incorporated into library and information services.

We must look at what we can do that is different, that can provide our readers and our patrons – our customers – with the information services they need in a manner that best suits them and, despite the fact that we do some things well, we must look at what we can stop doing and seek new products and services that will provide what our customers want. Society is changing at a drastic rate, and our customers expect us to change as well. I believe that entrepreneurial management, with its emphasis on the validity of change, is the key to providing the kinds of information products and services our publics are coming to us for. When we incorporate change and the change management process

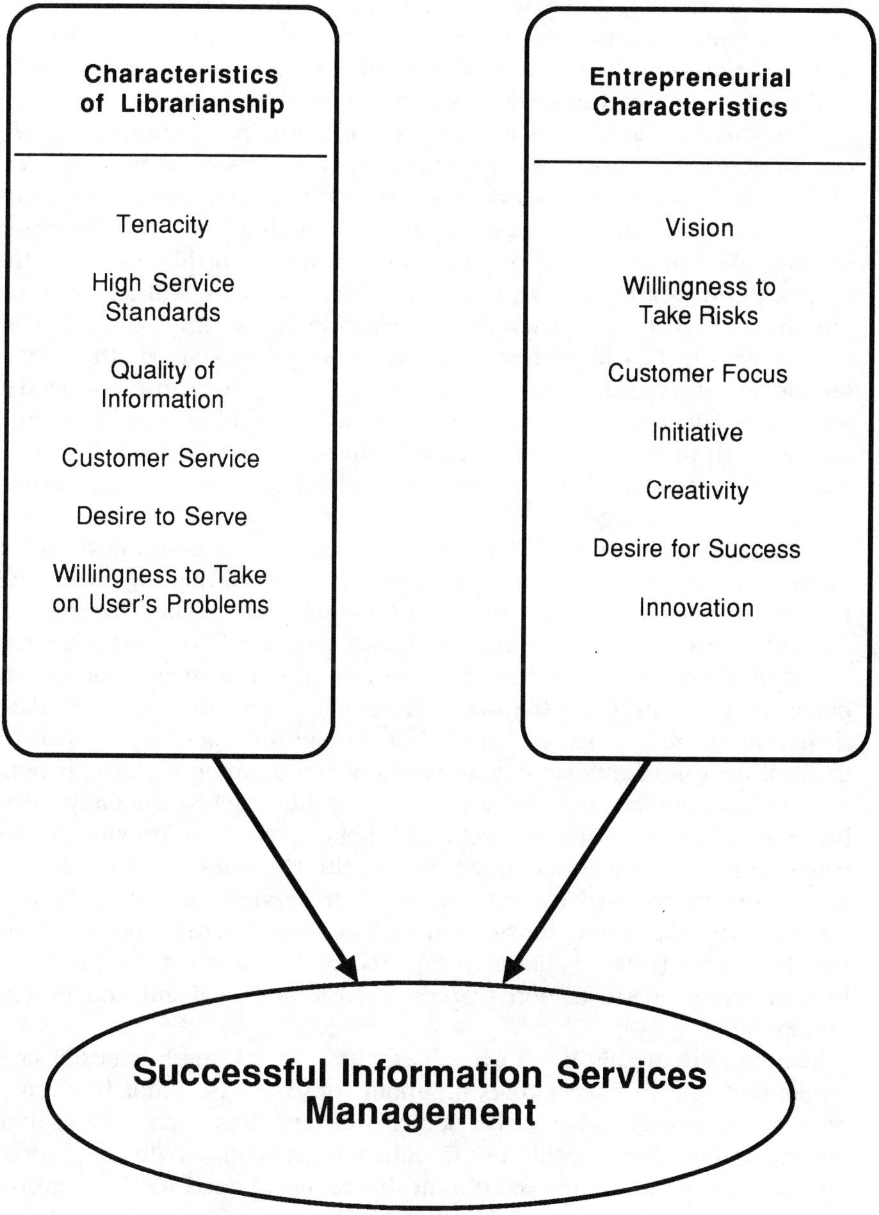

**Characteristics
of Librarianship**

Tenacity

High Service
Standards

Quality of
Information

Customer Service

Desire to Serve

Willingness to Take
on User's Problems

**Entrepreneurial
Characteristics**

Vision

Willingness to
Take Risks

Customer Focus

Initiative

Creativity

Desire for Success

Innovation

**Successful Information Services
Management**

Figure 1

into our work, and when we provide our services from a recognizable entrepreneurial perspective, we will find our place in society enhanced, and our profession will command the attention and respect it has always aspired to have but has never been able to claim.

Nevertheless, the book is not only about librarianship. Indeed, its very conception grew from a desire to take the strengths of librarianship and offer them to information services at large, so that all information services – regardless of format, content or delivery method – will be increased in value. We all know the popular perceptions about librarianship: that its practitioners are society's true detectives, that they will all but move mountains to get the reader the information he or she needs. Beyond this, however, it is important to think about how some of the characteristics of librarianship, and particularly its strengths, can be applied in other areas of information services. It is my contention here, of course, that it is through an entrepreneurial approach to information services management that those strengths can be transferred into the information services arena at large.

What are these strengths? Obviously, there is the determination just referred to, but that is only part of what I like to call the 'high standards' framework that makes up the basic foundations of librarianship. Its strengths are derived from an understanding of the theories of 'ideal' librarianship. When practised in the real world, of course, many barriers prevent librarians from attaining the high standards their professionalism sets for them, but they nevertheless *aspire* to reach them. If we can take these standards and match them up with the benefits of entrepreneurial management from other fields (notably from business and the for-profit sector), I believe we can provide a two-way exchange that will benefit all parties: the librarians, who will be able to use entrepreneurial tools to move their services and their libraries forward, and the other information services practitioners, who will use the high standards of librarianship to enable them to achieve the highest levels of satisfaction that their customers demand and deserve (Figure 1).

The genesis of this book goes back many years, for I honestly can't remember when I wasn't thinking about these things, about how entrepreneurs seemed to have the secret that we librarians – and other information workers – could use to enhance the work we do and, indeed, be better at it and at the same time be acknowledged for having done it. However, much of this work began to come into focus not many years ago, when I was serving as President of the Special Libraries Association, for part of my emphasis during that term of office was to attempt to articulate the differences between special librarianship and other types of librarianship. I wasn't always successful, but the concept of 'entrepreneurial librarianship' kept coming up. During that time, for example, I came across a couple of items in my readings, which seemed to address this issue. The thematic direction of these articles led me into much stimulating and provocative thought about these matters, and how they affect what we do as information services practitioners.

The first article was an opinion piece that conveyed considerable anxiety that the library community (that is, librarianship as a whole, not any particular 'type' of librarianship) seemed to be increasingly concerned with such things as marketing, benchmarking, downsizing and the like. It suggested that these concepts, related to management and the business community, aren't good for librarianship. Strategic planning, especially, was seen as a particularly nefarious technique, something that could lead us away from the higher purposes usually associated with librarianship. Librarians, the writer seemed to be saying, shouldn't tarnish themselves by using the methods and techniques that are used in the business world.

The second piece warned that doctors, by becoming more like 'entrepreneurs' (as some were seen to be doing), are in danger of demeaning themselves, that their respected position in society is likely to be compromised if they become too involved in entrepreneurial activities. The point was made that such activities could lead to the government – and society – treating physicians 'as entrepreneurs rather than as professionals'. The obvious implication, of course, was that 'entrepreneur' and 'professional' could not coexist in the same person. The two characterizations were seen as different, as being at opposite ends of the social spectrum, and the article seemed to be saying that one is good and one is bad. Physicians, it was pointed out, are engaged in 'a special calling ... They have different and higher duties than even the most ethical businessman.'

When I read that I began to wonder if we weren't ourselves responsible for some of the lack of success we seem so concerned about. Do we see ourselves as engaged in some 'higher calling', a vocation that puts us above the mere earning of a living and the making of a contribution? Are we afraid that if we adopt the efficiency, effectiveness and energy of the successful entrepreneur, we will somehow cease to be the ennobled, exalted paragons of virtue we've assumed ourselves to be throughout our professional history? Are we afraid the taint of 'entrepreneurism' will somehow prevent us from being the admired moral leaders we've been led to believe others think we are? Or that we ourselves think we are?

This may sound a little extreme, but it isn't far off the mark for some librarians. At the time I was confronting these issues, I was concerned with special librarianship, and that was where I put my emphasis. I pointed out that special librarians have been practising entrepreneurial librarianship for decades, and that they are very good at it. Special librarians understand the value of proactive information management, of relating their work to the mission of whatever parent organization or entity supports the unit they manage, of positioning themselves so that their libraries and information centers – and by definition the people who manage them – are supported in order to do the work they need to do. Those who manage and lead in the organizations where special librarians work are required to think entrepreneurially and special librarians think entrepreneurially, too. It's the way they function (and survive) in *their* environment.

That, it seems to me, is one of the primary differences between specialized librarianship and other branches of the library and information services profession, especially when we recognize that all forms of specialized librarianship and information services are what we call 'special' librarianship. Special librarians are part of somebody else's turf, and that turf is not necessarily a library or educational institution (although it can be, as when special librarians work in specific or particular departments or subject areas in public libraries or academic libraries). It was Ferguson and Mobley who first identified this as a distinguishing characteristic of specialized librarianship, and since their work in this area I have frequently quoted them and looked to this idea for help in molding much of my thinking about information service work. And, it is interesting to note, many others in special librarianship now recognize that special librarians are employees first and librarians second (Ferguson and Mobley, 1984, p. 97). It is an important perspective from which to approach entrepreneurial librarianship.

As for that editorial comment about strategic planning, at the time I was offended and felt that it was an insult to professional library managers who are attempting to run their libraries in the most efficient and effective manner. Yes, the concept does come from the business community, but what's wrong with that? In this day and age, any organization (whether public, private, profit, non-profit or not-for-profit) must engage seriously in strategic planning or there won't be anything a decade or so down the road to plan for. We in the library and information services profession have not been particularly adept at strategic planning (although most of our professional associations seem to be continuously engaged in serious and ongoing strategic planning in one form or another), and as we face our future, we must recognize that it is in effective planning that we will have our strength and our success.

This idea is not original with me and is, in fact, supported by others. W. David Penniman, for example, formerly the President of the Council on Library Resources, has spoken frequently about these matters and has often called for 'the pre-eminence of strategy over technology' (Penniman, 1992, p. 40). Paul Evans Peters, too, has taken the concept of planning for librarianship and moved it even further into the realm of management reality, for he declares that it is librarians themselves who can lead their communities into the successes that are waiting for them in the information age: 'The fact is librarians and libraries are ahead of the constituents they serve in exploring the opportunities and challenges of the Information Age' (Peters, 1995, p. 32). But Peters is very quick to observe that library managers and the facilities they are responsible for must go to their communities to determine what the communities want:

> We need to derive the future of the library from the future of its community. Most libraries are already proficient at arguing for investments in modern information technologies that will improve their own productivity. But many libraries are now learning to solicit funding based on their ability to advance their *communities'* objectives. (Peters, 1995, p. 33)

In effect, Peters and Penniman are recommending that all libraries and all information services enterprises must do what special librarians have been doing all along: they must go to their *customers*, and determine from *them* how the information services they provide affect *their* lives. This is the very essence of entrepreneurial librarianship, and it is a concept whose time has come. We do ourselves and our employers a disservice if we ignore the potential and value of strategic planning in the work we do.

So it seems important that we who work in information services should recognize the value of the entrepreneurial approach, and link it to the strategic planning and strategic management that are basic to the success of the organizations we work for. Should not strategic planning and strategic management be basic in the provision of information services? Of course they should, and that is why this book and the others in this series have come into being.

Certainly, the ideas put forward in this book have developed over many years, and it is appropriate to acknowledge some of the colleagues who are so encouraging in the work I do. Andrew Berner, my business partner and close friend, never ceases to amaze me with his good humor and his intelligent understanding of the complicated subjects we deal with in our profession. Beth Duston, a strategic partner with me in many consultations, is a tower of business acumen, and to my way of thinking, no one knows as much about entrepreneurial librarianship as she does. To the two of them, I respectfully dedicate this book and thank them for their work with me over these many years.

I also, as I developed my ideas, had good conversations with and received much support from David R. Bender, Miriam A. Drake, Joseph J. Fitzsimmons, Carol L. Ginsburg, Emily R. Mobley, Meg Paul, W. David Penniman, Martha P. B. Schweitzer and Ann J. Wolpert. Additionally, Ann Lawes, Marisa Urgo, and my niece Anne Trefz, have spent many hours talking with me about these subjects, and I respect their opinions and ideas greatly. I thank all of these people for their continued interest, and for sharing their thoughts with me.

At Bowker-Saur, too, I am supported in much of this effort, especially as we begin to build this series beyond my own writings. Val Skelton and Geraldine Turpie and others on the editorial staff at Maypole House are invaluable colleagues. They are steadfast in their kindness, and I very much appreciate all that they do for me and for the work we are attempting to do together.

Finally, two technical points should be made. First, some comment is required about the terms 'entrepreneurial' and 'intrapreneurial', particularly as they are used in this book. By now the latter term has entered into the language of management, thanks to the work of Gifford Pinchot III. In his book, Pinchot (1985) made a distinction between entrepreneurial and intrapreneurial work, his distinction being primarily that, as one writer in the field has suggested, intrapreneurship is defined as the taking in charge of an innovation by an employee or other individual working *under the control of an enterprise*. In other words, the intrapreneur is an entrepreneur who works for someone else. Obviously, then, in the information services context the entrepreneur must by definition be an intrapreneur (unless he or she is an independent information broker or consultant), as the ultimate 'benefits' from that 'entrepreneurial' work will accrue to the organization, company or enterprise under whose control he or she works. Nevertheless, in this text it has occasionally been necessary to interweave the two words, so to speak, because a reference to an 'entrepreneurial' activity fits into a discussion of an 'intrapreneurial' situation, or vice versa. I have attempted to adhere to Pinchot's distinctions in this book, but to avoid confusion I should state that – although one word is sometimes used in a context in which the other is being discussed – the intrapreneur is an entrepreneurially thinking employee who is part of another organization, and not an independent practitioner.

Secondly, I should point out that although direct quotations from the literature are cited, there are many occasions where I refer to people who have been interviewed in two of the publications which are produced by our company. *InfoManage: The International Management Newsletter for the Information Services Executive* has a monthly feature called 'The Information Interview,' in which a prominent leader in the information services field describes his or her work and some facet of that work which is relevant to the subject under discussion. *The One-Person Library: A Newsletter for Librarians and Managers* also publishes occasional 'profiles.' For both of these newsletters, I am responsible for interviewing these people and writing the articles. Therefore, for many references in this book to particular people, or discussions of their ideas, there are no 'formal' citations, as the information was gleaned in the interview or profile which appeared (usually in a different form) in those publications. Obviously, however, if the interview or profile is quoted directly, it is so cited. In both cases, I am grateful to these people for allowing me to interview them and for contributing both to our newsletters and to this book by sharing with me their insights about the management of information services.

Guy St Clair
New York
31 July 1995

References

Drucker, Peter F. *Innovation and Entrepreneurship*. New York: Harper & Row, 1985.

Drucker, Peter F. *Managing for the Future: the 1990s and Beyond*. New York: Truman Talley Books, 1992.

Ferguson, Elizabeth and Mobley, Emily R. *Special Libraries at Work*. Hamden, Connecticut: The Shoe String Press, 1984.

Penniman, David R. 'Shaping the future: the Council on Library Resources helps to fund change.' *Library Journal*, 117 (17), October 15, 1992.

Peters, Paul Evan. 'Information age avatars.' *Library Journal*, 120 (5), March 15, 1995.

Foreword

Guy St Clair is a prolific writer who is well versed in the corporate library/information service milieu. He has always spoken many truths for those who might listen. His books on the various facets of management are fast becoming classics in the field. Guy also has an uncanny sense of timing in that he always presents a topic just as the profession needs it the most. This book, *Entrepreneurial Librarianship*, follows his traditional sense of timing because it comes at a time when the paradigm of librarianship is shifting, regardless of the environment in which it is practised. Due to the extent of the changes necessary to provide effective information services and the information contained within this book to help a reader make these changes, this book is his most important one to date.

The need to approach library management from an entrepreneurial business perspective is important, perhaps vital is a better choice of word, whether the information facility is in a corporate, academic, public or school setting. Only the gradients of such a perspective may differ. Accountability, planning, risk-taking and creative approaches are features of every environment. Every successful information services manager should not only be versed with these topics, but such attributes should be a hallmark of one's management. Regardless of the depth of good service orientation, the best as one knew it in the past is no longer good enough. In this day when continuous quality improvement is demanded as the *modus operandi* regardless of the environment, librarians do not have the luxury of managing using old paradigms.

The discussion on the shifting paradigms is important for gaining a perspective on what has happened. The sections on accountability, performance and performance measurement are classic Guy St Clair. The segments of the book which discuss the importance of risk-taking are critical to understanding the shifting paradigms. Unfortunately librarianship has the reputation of being risk-adverse. Making a successful transition to the new paradigms requires a fundamental change in the profession's traditional approach to risk.

In the Introduction to the Information Services Management series, Guy St Clair writes: '... Entrepreneurial Librarianship ... would seem to be limited to the library profession, but in fact the book will offer information and guidance of use to anyone working in the information services field who is willing to incorporate entrepreneurial thinking into his or her work'. The book is here at hand and it succeeds in doing exactly what the author envisions.

Emily R. Mobley
Dean of Libraries
Purdue University
West Lafayette, IN

Chapter One
Entrepreneurial librarianship

For some time, librarians and other information services professionals have been thinking about entrepreneurial management. There exists in our work a splendid tension that drives everything we do, and at the beginning of our careers we are delighted to have the opportunity to bring our expertise and enthusiasm to bear on the information problems our customers bring to us.

It is, alas, a short-lived tension which for many is sublimated early in their professional careers. Upon entering the field, most information workers are anxious to provide the highest levels of service to their clients, and they approach their work with remarkable enthusiasm and commitment. Unfortunately, after they have been employed for a while, many of these bright, enthusiastic new librarians find that the managerial and intellectual 'climate' in the organizations where they work is not particularly conducive to providing those high levels of service. In fact, whether these organizations are 'libraries' as such, or attached to a parent organization, they are frequently weighed down by processes and procedures that are barriers to excellence. The tension develops when the information worker's standards of excellence conflict with organizational lassitude. Its true beauty comes when the employee is energized to reach beyond the usual inhibitions of the organization to provide best information services anyway. In each of these situations it is entrepreneurial thinking that drives the employee, and when the information worker is inspired to reach for a level of service he or she knows can best serve the user, entrepreneurial librarianship is at work.

Managers of libraries and other information services want to think entrepreneurially. Librarianship is not a business, and most of us recognize that the management of library and information services can never be organized as business management is organized (unless, of course, the information enterprise is a specifically designated commercial one). Yet the library product cannot be dismissed as merely another ephemeral bureaucratic service delivered by practitioners when convenient. To meet the needs of users, library management must now be driven by the same qualities that characterize a successful business operation or any other enterprise: *responsibility, performance, and control*. Entrepreneurial thinking, which brings an innovative attitude to the process, combines with responsibility, performance and control to enable the effective information services manager to provide the highest levels of information service to the users (Figure 1.1).

According to many in library work today, attitude has much to do with whether library and information services management is successful or

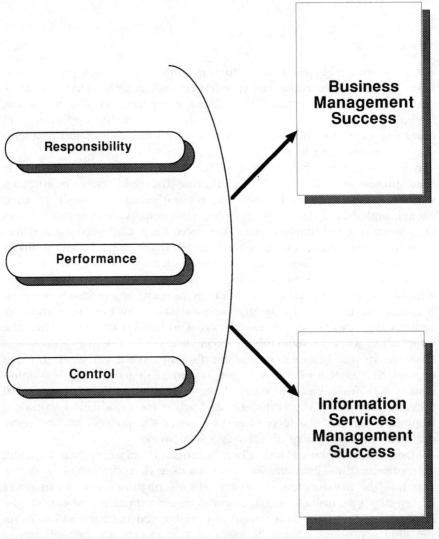

Figure 1.1

not. Excellence of service begins with one's approach to one's work, the perspective from which one views the information function in the community or organization. It also includes a disposition toward service, a willingness to provide the user with whatever it is he or she seeks, and a bias toward care. These are all characteristics which, for at least a hundred years, have applied to librarianship and the provision of information services and products.

This willingness to take on the user's problem is a defining principle for people who choose information services as a career. To be able to work with the user to achieve an acceptable solution to the problem, whatever that problem might be, has been a notable and dignifying attribute of the profession. Today, however, many information workers simply do not have the opportunity to be as useful to their clients as they would like to be. For a variety of reasons, as society changes and libraries and other service professions come under pressure to 'prove' their value to the communities and organizations that support them, the fear of losing this disposition towards service is very real. The best solution, for all concerned, is entrepreneurial librarianship.

How do I define 'entrepreneurial librarianship'? In fact, the concept has been incorporated into the literature of this particular branch of information services for more than a decade. As early as 1984, Beth Duston was writing about the 'intrapreneurial' librarian, taking a page from Gifford Pinchot's book and applying the intrapreneurial concept to information services. After a couple of years, articles were appearing with some regularity in the *Journal of Library Administration* as well as other professional journals, in all of which the authors attempted – often successfully – to connect innovation, creativity and entrepreneurial management to library and information services. Certainly in the last few years, the entrepreneurial/innovative concepts espoused in the work of thinkers like Peter Drucker, Tom Peters, John Nesbitt, Joel Barker and others have frequently been translated into the library/information services management literature, most notably by writers like Herbert S. White, Joanne R. Euster, Miriam A. Drake, Forest Woody Horton Jr. and James M. Matarazzo, to name but a few. So there is definitely a perception that there is a place for entrepreneurial management within library and information services. Whether that perception evolves into a reality remains to be seen.

Our purpose here is to attempt to link the concept of entrepreneurial management with librarianship as a specific service discipline, and then to further link the components of entrepreneurial librarianship with the various activities that make up the information services field at large. For librarianship, despite its long and distinguished history as a service profession, can no longer be considered a 'standalone' service activity. As society moves into the twenty-first century, librarianship is but one subset of a multitude of service activities that are more rightly described

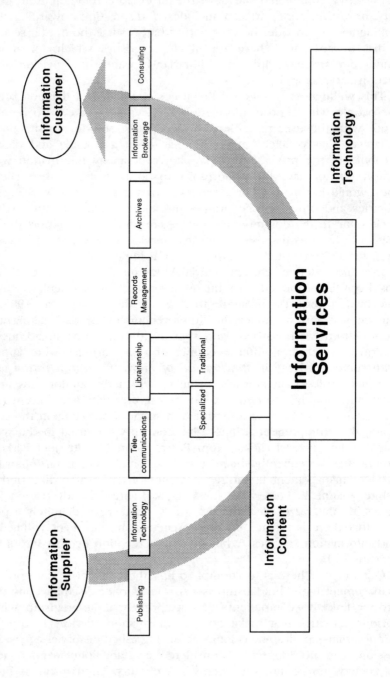

Figure 1.2

as information services. Such services are known by a great multiplicity of names but primarily they embody, in addition to librarianship, such information delivery activities as records management, organizational or corporate archives, information brokerage, information resources management, publishing and consulting. Information technology, the development of software and hardware, telecommunications, and electronic publishing fit equally well into an information services scheme, and the futurists of information services – embodied in such groups as the United States Federal Government (in its attention to the development of a National Information Infrastructure), the 'G7' nations, the group of seven leading economic group nations (in that body's attention to the development of a global information infrastructure), the Information Futures Institute, various other 'think tanks' and research/discussion groups, and various professional associations – all come together under one framework which pulls together all efforts to deliver information to the people who seek it.

Information itself is now defined very broadly, and while specific and traditional approaches to information delivery continue, among some information leaders the move to a more integrated perspective is wholly appropriate. In the specialized research and business community, for example, information is anything workers need to know in order to do their work. Thus 'information' can include such items as customer records, information from and about suppliers, information about budgets, financial results, R&D reports and so forth. At the same time, and of special interest for workers in libraries, the list includes external information that workers must have available in order to achieve their workplace objectives, and in most organizations it is the library which is usually charged to provide external information. As a result of this new thinking about how information is defined, many information services managers and consultants, even vendors, have begun to organize their work not around the way in which the information is stored, or the medium through which it is delivered, but around the end-user and the use to which it will be put. These people are all seeking to achieve one goal: to provide the information their customers seek. Under this framework, information services and information services management, as a discipline and specific field of study, is structured (Figure 1.2).

William H. Davidow and Michael S. Malone put this concept in perspective when they describe the 'virtual corporation,' for in their description it becomes clear that the idea of integrated information is not necessarily a new phenomenon: it is new only to those information services workers who are only now willing to recognize it and embrace it. Davidow and Malone credit Peter Drucker (1985, p. 25) for his attention to the restructuring of the organization around information, and they quote Rosabeth Moss Kanter's (1986, p. 86) assertion that in some organizations the MIS (the computer-based management information system) can be so integrated that it can provide entrepreneurial/

intrapreneurial activities for the organization. In the information-based organization, according to Davidow and Malone (1992, p. 174), 'information becomes a vital management support system as the application of information technology is expanded. . . .' This management support system will eventually include all information, internal and external. It is an organization that is based on integrated information services.

Perceptions of entrepreneurship

The entrepreneur has not always been a welcome member of society, and as recently as the 1970s most references to the entrepreneurial temperament were, if not condemnatory, at least somewhat accusatory and at best condescending. It seemed that there was something not quite respectable about the entrepreneur, as if thinking about things differently made one suspect, not quite part of the team or the group. The way to success (so we were told) was to follow the established norm, to 'not make waves,' and especially, if we wanted to enter a solid, secure profession like librarianship, to avoid doing anything that would make people notice us.

What is it about entrepreneurial thinking that makes people nervous? There are a variety of attributes ascribed to entrepreneurs, and depending on the point of view of the person making the list, 'individuality, determination, persistence, vision for new ideas and opportunities, flexibility and a willingness to take calculated risks' can all be identified (Cottam, p. 29). These characteristics may or may not be seen as positive, depending on the organizational culture in which the librarian finds himself or herself. With enthusiastic young people just coming from graduate school, the more seasoned manager often has to work hard to maintain a tolerant outlook. Certainly some of us, in our early years, were a source of some anguish for our supervisors. I remember one boss, the head of the reference department in a fairly large public library, for whom I worked. In exasperation she one day called me aside to tell me that I was 'driving her crazy.' Apparently I had not yet learned to temper my enthusiastic demands for change in the department with any reasoned analysis of what the results of some of my proposed changes might be for others who worked there. Fortunately, this manager encouraged my free-thinking approach to reference services, and even after this uncharacteristic outburst she reverted to being the kind and encouraging mentor she had been up to that point. Yet even the most enthusiastic new staff member must be guided and mentored, and to this day I appreciate the admonition.

On the other hand, from some points of view, 'entrepreneurs are perceived to be risk-taking innovators, individualistic, believers in themselves and in their own competence regardless of the views of others, and as often as not stubborn, selfish, insensitive to the concerns of others, at least when those concerns get in their way, and sometimes arrogant and ruthless.' (White, p. 11) There are, indeed, those who drive themselves hard, who believe that their role in the organization or community is to figure out how to do things better (which they often define as 'differently'), and they are, indeed, difficult employees. For their managers and supervisors, the problem becomes one of encouragement within the framework of organizational or departmental achievement, and as long as organizational goals have been clearly established and the innovative activity is engaged in as part of the accomplishment of those goals, the achievements of the employee, despite the arrogance and ruthlessness, are worth the pain.

A current example of this phenomenon has to do with the extreme amount of time that must nowadays be devoted to working with the Internet. Of course we are all very happy that the Internet exists and that it can be used to access information tools that simply were not available (or not available without large expenditures of funds) in an earlier time. Nevertheless, those librarians who are drawn to the Internet for hours of experimentation must be quickly drawn back to reality by an encouraging but stern supervisor, for unless an organizational or departmental context for the experimentation is established, the other work of the department simply will not be done. If the supervisor can establish a structure into which the innovative activity will fit, the employee will be happy and the department will benefit from his/her particular innovative attributes.

Entrepreneurs are most often identified as risk takers, people willing 'to take risks in organizing, managing and directing an enterprise,' and intrapreneurs (who are the primary entrepreneurs of librarianship, a distinction based on their continuing to work within the organization and pursuing entrepreneurial objectives for the benefit of the organization, rather than leaving the organization to work externally) do not necessarily take risks that are irrational or dangerous to their work. According to Cottam,

> They assume a willingness to risk their dreams and ideas, even their job security for the opportunity to figure out ways to achieve – not for goals themselves but for what it takes to get there. On the other hand, the risks are usually calculated. Intrapreneurs anticipate obstacles to reduce the risks. They plan and avoid high risk situations. They eschew uncontrollable circumstances and work to minimize the risks within a defined area of endeavor. In the balance, careful risk has its compensation. (Cottam, p. 30–31)

Who in librarianship would be such a risk taker? Certainly in this day and age of limited resources and increasing demand, public librarians are not expected to take risks, and yet some do. Mark Merrifield in York, Pennsylvania, is a library manager/leader who sees his role as one of encouraging risk among his staff, and it never occurs to him to question the appropriateness of entrepreneurial activity in a 'library' organization. And if risk-taking is a characteristic of the entrepreneur, Merrifield is nothing if not entrepreneurial. At the Martin Memorial Library, where Merrifield is Director of Marketing and Development, a conscious decision has been made to provide consultation services, information brokerage services and similar information activities, for a fee, to the research and specialized libraries in the geographical area. Such activities of course run against the usual preconceptions about what a public library 'should' be doing, and the library is continuing to do those things and to offer usual public library services without fees, for the usual library patrons. But for an identified market that is willing, indeed anxious, to pay for a different level of service, Merrifield takes the risk, and the library, as a result, is required to receive only fifty percent of its operating revenue from public funds. So in this case taking the risk pays off and, as far as the public funding authorities are concerned, the message is one that the library staff and its Board of Directors are happy with.

This is an attitude that connects the delivery of information services with some responsibility for support. 'We're telling the funding authorities that we're not on the public dole,' Merrifield said. 'We're telling the people who make library funding decisions for the State of Pennsylvania, for the City of York, and for York and Adams Counties (which we also serve), that we recognize our own responsibility. We have to earn the support we obtain from the public authorities and we're glad to do it.'

Another view of entrepreneurs usually characterizes them as being good at starting organizations, but not necessarily good at managing them. In fact, according to White, in the general perception of entrepreneurs, 'their knack, their accomplishment, and their success comes from starting organizations, not for managing mature ones,' and since libraries 'are, after all, very mature organizations,' entrepreneurs have not been especially successful in librarianship. White paints a discouraging picture for the budding service entrepreneur seeking to find a profession where his or her particular talents might be appreciated:

> They [libraries] have a hardening of decision arteries brought about not only by the risk avoidance tendencies of many librarians, but by a preference for minimal or no changes by the library's clientele, be these academic faculty members, special library users whose preconceptions come from what they have seen as university students, or the public library patrons heavily skewed toward children and the elderly. All are groups that have an affinity toward the library just as it is. Individuals who like the library just as it is do not tend to try to change it. They just ignore it and as we already know from a variety of research investigations the existence of an inadequate library does not pose an insurmountable barrier. Users adapt to poor service, find other approaches to information, or pretend they never needed the information in the first place. (White, p. 13)

Such resistance is, of course, the very kind of barrier a Mark Merrifield would encounter, and the entrepreneurial success of his operation is characterized through a clear explanation and understanding of what the benefits to the user group are going to be. In a related type of situation, in Washington DC, a government agency with responsibility for distributing certain information products and services to a clearly identified customer base was threatened with closure, not because there was not enough information to distribute or because there was no market for it, but because, with approximately sixty percent of its potential market working in laboratories and research institutes on the west coast of America, which operates on a three-hour time differential from the east coast, few requests for information were coming from the west coast. The manager of the information unit discovered, through his own observations, that although the unit 'officially' closed at 4:30 each afternoon (a time established for the benefit of the service employees), few telephones were answered after about 3:30, meaning that anyone on the west coast had to call between the hours of 9:30 am and 12:30 pm. These customers were obviously adapting in some way to poor service, for they were not coming to the agency for the information it could provide.

A simple experiment of asking certain employees to work longer hours for a defined period of two weeks provided enough documentation to support a change in working hours for the agency, and although some employees balked, when they were apprised of the fact that the unit would be forced to close unless its hours of operation were matched to service requirements from all customers, agreement was reached and service hours were extended. For the employees, having a job – even one with hours that they did not wholeheartedly support – was far preferable to being without. Their manager had to demonstrate to them that their reason for being there was more important than their work schedules, but the evidence he produced was irrefutable, a point not lost on the employees and their union representatives when the decision had to be made.

But entrepreneurial librarianship is more than innovation, risk taking, and what might be called the 'start-up' mentality. It also relates to the use of innovation in the achievement of the information service's goals, and in most situations that goal is to deliver the highest levels of information to the customer. For many library managers, barriers to such service delivery are found within the organizational hierarchy, the community, or the way in which their employees have been recruited, and for them the entrepreneurial route is the only way they can achieve what they need to.

This is precisely the direction Forest Woody Horton Jr. (1994) envisages as he encourages librarians to 'extend their domain'. Horton presents six 'arguable propositions' that form the basis of his thesis that there are a variety of opportunities for librarians and other information workers to enhance their work and their contribution to the organizations that employ them. The first two of Horton's propositions, that information has become 'the key transforming resource' in today's society and that organizations are undergoing 'fundamental and radical structural transformations in order to cope with and adapt to external changes,' lead to four further assumptions that underscore the role of the entrepreneurial information manager. The first, that organizations are becoming 'far more information intensive, and are demanding a far higher degree of information literacy than ever before,' provides an unparalleled opportunity for the entrepreneurial information services manager to take his unit's products and services to the customers. This opportunity is, however, threatened by another assumption: that librarians, while being 'the premier information experts in organizational settings' are, in fact, victims of distressing stereotypical prejudices that inhibit their full success. For the entrepreneurial librarian, such prejudices are ripe for refutation.

Another of Horton's propositions is practically a call to arms for entrepreneurial thinkers in the information field, for he asserts that 'if librarians

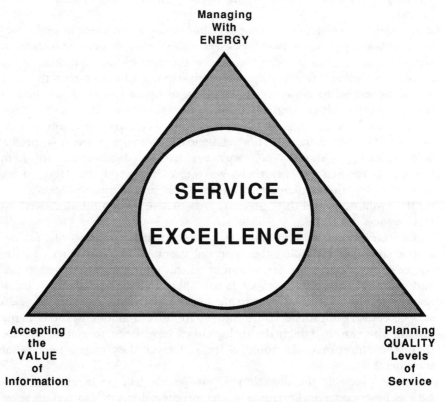

Figure 1.3

and other information professionals are to fill the hundreds of thousands of emerging new jobs and positions that are located outside the library domain (in non-traditional settings, as they are sometimes called), there must be a shift in primary focus from describing, organizing and cataloging books as physical entities or information containers, to planning and managing the information requirements and needs of decision makers in organizations in which they serve.' Finally, Horton encourages librarians and other information workers to 'move out of the traditional library domain and move into other organizational domains, espousing and fostering their competencies as generalists whose skills are critical and in great demand – much like the lawyer or accountant or personnel specialist is found throughout the organization wherever there is a need for their particular specialized competencies' (Horton, p. 2).

Clearly, Horton has tapped into an entrepreneurial spirit for information services management, for his admonitions demonstrate exactly the point of view that leads to an acceptance of the value of the information services unit within the organization or community of which it is a part, and at the same time provides a direction for the information services manager in his or her thinking about how quality levels of service can be provided. It is this kind of leadership that will bring information managers into positions of value in their organizations as we move into a new century, and what is being described as a 'second era' of information services.

This providing of excellence in the delivery of information services and products to an identified body of information customers is a splendid continuum, and it begins with the acceptance of the value of the information services unit, and the finding of a direction for planning quality levels of service. In the final analysis, what today's information services manager is seeking is nothing less than that excellence of service. Extra energy or effort is thus required when the barriers of the workplace, the organization or community, the society, or even of the customers themselves, (in their expectations of what they will or will not receive from the information services operation), impede the achievement of that excellence. An entrepreneurial approach enables the information services manager to provide the services the customers want (Figure 1.3).

References

Cottam, Keith M. 'Professional Identity and "Intrapreneurial" Behavior.' *Journal of Library Administration*, 8 (1) Spring, 1987.

Davidow, William H. and Malone, Michael S. 'Rethinking Management.' *The Virtual Corporation*. New York: HarperCollins, 1992.

Drucker, Peter F. *Innovation and Entrepreneurship: Practice and Principles*. New York: Harper & Row, 1985.

Drucker, Peter F. 'Tomorrow's Restless Managers.' *Industry* Week, April 18, 1988.

Horton, Forest Woody Jr. *Extending the Librarian's Domain: A Survey of Emerging Occupation Opportunities for Librarians and Information Professionals*. Washington DC: Special Libraries Association, 1994.

Kanter, Rosabeth Moss. 'The New Managerial Work.' *Harvard Business Review*, November/December, 1989.

White, Herbert S. 'Entrepreneurship and the Library Profession.' *Journal of Library Administration*, 8 (1), Spring, 1987.

Chapter Two
Risk-taking in the information services environment

The business of information services management has become an entrepreneur's dream. There is so much going on and so much interest is being shown by so many people in participating in the development of new products and services that today's information services professional is almost by default an entrepreneur. Every news magazine, every newspaper, and just about any 'public-interest' radio or television station carries report after report about how new technologies are enabling members of society to gather more and more information and, when they don't know how to do so for themselves, to learn how, or to find those who can gather it for them. Such a 'Wild-West' environment is naturally going to bring forth entrepreneurs eager to participate, to capitalize on the almost universal interest in information activities and services. At the same time, economic conditions and the unsettled environment of the workplace has loosed upon society a plethora of people determined to control their own livelihoods, who eagerly embrace the entrepreneurial drive as their motivating influence.

Obviously, with the field of information services made up of such varied components, the prevailing atmosphere is one of enthusiasm, excitement and continual change. For librarians, with their highly developed historical and cultural tradition of service, the prevailing mood is tailor-made for moving into a new stage of professional development: if the library community truly desires to give more than lip service to its acknowledged goal of superior service for all comers, the acceptance of and the move towards entrepreneurial librarianship can provide a splendid opportunity to fulfil those desires. In addition, the establishment of an entrepreneurial underpinning will lead to a recognition that librarianship is, at long last, the quality service profession it was always meant to be.

In moving in this direction, however, entrepreneurial librarianship will be taking to itself the standards that are used as evaluative measures in other entrepreneurial fields, and responsibility, accountability and effectiveness measurement will enter into the library profession in a way never before experienced. Librarians and the services and products they provide will be judged as they have never been judged before. Nevertheless, librarians will thereby be creating a model for the other branches of information provision that fall under the broad umbrella of information services. Entrepreneurial librarianship will bring to the entire field of information services management a level of quality service and customer response that will raise overall standards. It is not a prospect to be dismissed lightly.

If we accept Drucker's (1985) proposition that entrepreneurship 'rests on a theory of economy and society [that] sees change as normal and healthy, and sees the major task in society as doing something different rather than doing better what is already being done', it is no coincidence that, in information services, the concepts of entrepreneurship are linked to strategic planning. And by connecting Drucker's idea with that of David Ferriero and T.L. Wilding, that strategic planning assumes that change is both inevitable and desirable, that 'organizations exist in a dynamic relationship with their environments, and that for an organization to thrive, it must be in a constant state of change in order to maintain a high degree of relevance' (Ferriero and Wilding, p. 2), it becomes clear that entrepreneurial librarianship is highly appropriate as a projection paradigm for future information services. Like much else in society today, information services and their management are drastically affected by constant change, and efforts to match service demands and customer expectations to what is available can be exceedingly frustrating for the manager. Entrepreneurial librarianship can provide a foundation upon which to build those information services.

I have stated that this book is an attempt to link the concepts of entrepreneurial management with librarianship and to further link the components of entrepreneurial librarianship with the information management activities that make up the information services field as a whole. What should be apparent is that the first entrepreneurial attribute – a willingness to take risks – is an essential characteristic of information services management, and always has been. Any study of librarianship as a customer-focused service profession will demonstrate that the truly successful librarian is one who takes risks. Not only that, he or she looks for risks, for built into every good library manager's agenda is an understanding of the concept that reaches for new and better ways to provide library services to ever-expanding and ever-changing customer groups. Not for nothing are public librarians forever studying marketing strategies or looking for new services to offer to newly identified population groups. Such service essentials are the core of librarianship, and they are only dissipated when organizational bureaucracy comes between the suppliers of the service and those for whom the services were designed in the first place, the patrons. When this happens the librarians soon become worn down and 'burnt out', and service to the customers suffers.

But the core is still there. The librarians *want* to provide the services: it's just that they are prevented from doing so. And when they are prevented too often, they become dispirited and inhibited, and soon their own service focus is compromised. It's a great loss to society when that happens, but it does happen, and it has happened so often over the past few generations that librarianship as a profession has itself been characterized as bureaucratic, rule driven and risk avoiding, but this is a depiction that does not hold up under examination. Had librarians over the years been allowed to express their natural service desires, the exciting ideals of service that can be so attractive in any group of graduate students entering the profession, the profession would not today be struggling with its so-called 'image problem'. Librarianship would be recognized for what it is: a customer-centered information services provider with the highest standards of both service and product for its identified constituencies.

But we cannot undo the past. What we can and must do is look to a future in which all information services take as their guiding principle the concepts of customer service that have for so long characterized librarianship as it was meant to be practiced. This means that information services managers (and practitioners) must be constantly looking for change, must recognize that it is through change that services become better and more satisfying to the customers, and that the change process, involving as it does an acceptance of a certain degree of risk, will be healthy and beneficial for all concerned.

Risk in the information environment

Risk and the management of risk have become so much a part of society today that the word no longer has the fearsome connotations it used to have, and the usual definition – i.e. a chance of encountering harm or loss, hazard or danger – is no longer even thought about. We all know what people are talking about when they refer to someone or something as being 'at risk', or when they refer to 'risk avoidance'. The possibility of loss, injury, disadvantage, or destruction, the threat of something bad happening is no longer defined: we simply refer to 'the risk'.

In information services, especially in librarianship, the concept comes into play as we think about the results of any particular decision or action. Often, simply putting the proposal under consideration into a 'worst-case scenario' framework can quickly establish the risk involved in the venture. For example, if the librarian in a small rural community, providing public library services with limited funds and limited staff support, decides to approach the local high school librarian to suggest a cooperative arrangement through which the public library would offer additional evening openings at the end of the school term, when the students are studying for their final examinations, in return for the school library's providing staff to keep the public library open, the risks can be identified right away and, in all likelihood the offer will not even be made. Although the idea seems to be a good one as far as the particular service group (the high school students) is concerned, it is not difficult to envisage the worst-case scenario: the librarian is taking a risk that, with the public library open longer, other people will also want to use it during those hours, will become accustomed to the idea, and will put pressure on the librarian to reorganize the hours of service to meet these new demands. She knows that she does not have the staff to support increased hours, and she also knows that the funding authorities would not authorize additional staff to work at the library, so she puts away her good idea and the students' special needs at exam time go unmet. She cannot take the risk.

There is also a second risk, for the high school library is managed by a single librarian with aides and students as support staff. There is no one for the high school librarian to send to the public library, and in any case, employees of the school district cannot work for the public library, which is part of the county administration, and vice versa. So here the risk is even more clear cut, and provides the librarian with her disappointing conclusion: why bother to ask the question – she would just be refused.

A happier scenario is not necessarily out of the question, however. As she thinks about the risks involved in her radical proposal, the community librarian might also do well to consider a 'best-case' scenario in which she might approach the parent/teacher group and asks for volunteers to supervise the library during the exam period, as she is willing to have the building open for use as a study hall for the students to work on their assignments, as long as library staff are not required to be there. The library will not be open to the public but will be reserved for the students for their particular use and will be advertised as such. By limiting the participants, she is limiting her risk.

This is a simple, fairly open-and-shut case. Most risk situations in the information services field are not quite so obviously resolved, and as librarians and other information services practitioners become more determined to provide the highest levels of service to their users, turning to a worst-case scenario is not always the solution. Sometimes the risks are not so obvious, or the 'worst case' turns on the revelation of some unknown fact or activity beyond the control of the librarian making the decision. It's easy enough for the information services manager in a private research institute to look at the advantages and disadvantages of setting up a fax-on-demand service for scientists who work in the same building as the information center; it's quite another matter when management decides that the service should be extended to scientists working at remote sites as well, and that in order to have some sort of control over the usage of the service, a charge-back system is required. What seemed like a good idea is suddenly a 'worst-case' situation, and the information services manager could not have anticipated this particular risk.

Peter F. Drucker is also worthy of attention in the discussion of risk. Drucker has identified three kinds of risk and, as he was writing about the non-profit organization, it is not difficult to transfer his idea into the library/information services field. In most cases, we think about risk because we have found an opportunity and we want to act on it, but what is required from the professional information services manager is an ability to determine the balance between opportunity and risk, to know when the opportunity should be taken or when the risk is just too great for there to be any possibility for success.

Drucker writes of the three kinds of risk: 'There is the risk we can afford to take. If it goes wrong, it is easily reversible with minor damage. Then there is the irreversible decision, when failure may do serious harm. Finally there is the decision where the risk is great but one cannot afford *not* to take it.' (Drucker, 1990, p. 123) All three types of risk are present in the library and information services profession. The first, in which the risk is one the librarian can afford to take, is of course the scenario the rural community librarian found herself in. What was the 'worst-case' scenario? Having volunteers run the library for those few evenings of the week while the students were studying for their examinations, with no additional staff to handle the extra housekeeping required, meant that the library would probably be untidy when the librarian arrived for work in the morning, materials would be misplaced and books misshelved, and of course setting such a precedent would mean that the service would be expected in the future, whenever exam time came around. Was this a problem? Was this a risk the librarian could take? Of course, because failure would be something that could be lived with. At worst there would be some disgruntled parents because the experiment wasn't continued, and perhaps some disappointed students because they had no place to study for their exams, but in the long run this was a risk that could be taken. If it went wrong it would be easily reversible and the damage minor.

The second type of risk that Drucker identifies is the irreversible decision, when failure may do serious harm, and this is exemplified by a scenario that is all too familiar to library managers. Installing any automation system in a library is a frightening experience, but even with the assurance and confidence gained over years of working with a system, when it becomes time to upgrade into a third- or fourth-generation system the level of stress is almost palpable. It *is* an irreversible decision, and one that will have to be lived with for a long time. Nevertheless, the very irreversibility of the decision makes it easier for the librarian or information services manager to handle this risk, for despite the 'serious harm' that failure might precipitate (and it would indeed be serious, particularly if the automation is second- or third-generation or later), the manager will have long ago decided that the benefits to be gained if the new system is installed properly far outweigh the disadvantages that will come to the organization if it fails.

Information services employees, especially librarians, are often inclined to think in terms of just how good a service or product can be, rather than in terms of worst-case scenarios, and despite their frustrations with bureaucratic and organizational obstacles they continue to harbor an inclination to attempt the third type of risk that Drucker identifies, where

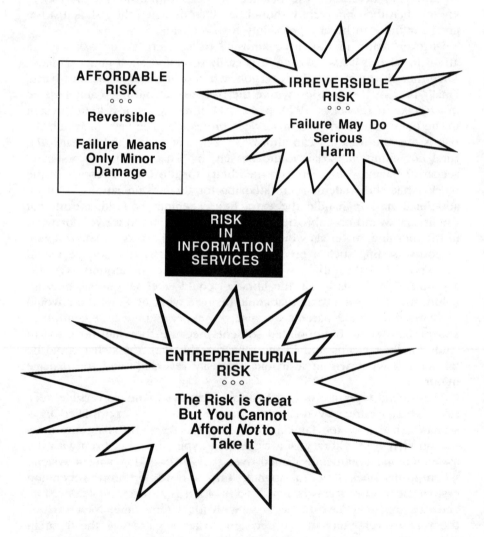

Figure 2.1 Adapted from Peter F. Drucker's Managing the Nonprofit Organization: Principles and Practices

the risk is great but one cannot afford *not* to take it (Figure 2.1). Think, for example, of an international research association which has accepted responsibility for the development and distribution of standards for, say, engineers and physicists who are developing highly sophisticated optical devices for the aeronautics industry. The various records of the many standards committees, communications between committee members and between the committees and the research association itself, collaboration documents, draft standards and approved standards continue to be distributed in hard copy. Despite the fact that most of these scientists have come to rely on the Internet and other electronic means for their other work, their activities with the organization in question are seriously hampered by their necessary reliance on the distribution of paper documents. Also, because of the work involved in producing paper copies of all documentation, the process has evolved into a costly and long-term one, with standards occasionally being in a 'draft' and 'unapproved' stage for several years at a time. This is clearly a situation in which the information services operation is going to be required to take a risk, and the risk is great, for much effort and a major allocation of resources will go into the research, development and installation of an electronic system that will meet the needs of the various users. The information staff will be required to become involved in pricing and setting out specifications for CD-ROM products, online distribution services, fax-on-demand, and a variety of other electronic access and distribution media that for most of them represent a major departure from their routine tasks. Nevertheless, in Drucker's terms it is a risk that the organization cannot afford *not* to take, simply because the people who are most affected by the information products and services emanating from the organization require electronic access. In fact, the organization's very survival now depends on the move toward an electronic information services program, for the development of standards and the production and distribution process cannot continue to operate as they have operated in the past. In this case there may well be years of struggle before the new system is perfected and before it is acceptable to all information stakeholders in the organization and its work, but to achieve its mission, which is to provide standards for the industry, the organization and its leaders are required to take the risk.

This last example illustrates the 'why' of risk in the information services community today, that in order to provide better services or to bring current services up to the level at which the library/information services managers feel should be offered, it is often necessary to look beyond the immediate danger, the possibility of harm that might result if the action is not taken. For librarians, service to the patrons overrides such considerations, especially in the context of planning future services and products, and risk taking is all the more acceptable as a part of one's managerial responsibilities – so much so that there are situations in which risk is not even acknowledged as an issue. Lois Weinstein, Director of the Medical Library Center of New York, is a case in point.

Weinstein manages a consortium that supports the work of (and is supported by) some seventy institutions. Created in 1959 to form an agency for the storage, retrieval and rapid dispersal of older medical literature, MLCNY, as it is known, exists to serve its customers, and Weinstein enthusiastically describes one of MLCNY's most recent projects, the organization and implementation of a sophisticated online system for its Union Catalog of Medical Periodicals. Approximately 750 libraries participate in the catalog, a unique bibliographic reference tool which provides bibliographic and location information for medical libraries in the middle Atlantic and northeastern United States. Recognizing that the Center was going to be in financial difficulty if something was not done to improve the way in which data were collected and distributed (30% of the institution's revenues came from the sale of the information collected), Weinstein put together a project that takes the Medical Library Center into the twenty-first century. As an entrepreneurial management effort her work was exemplary, although she did not necessarily see it that way. When asked, she simply replied that entrepreneurial librarianship is nothing more than a quest for *business* results: when you're making money, you stay in business; when you're losing money, you go out of business. In her organization, the predictions were that unless something was done to turn around some of the predicted loss of customers, MLCNY was going to lose money on its operations, and that would be a bad business situation even though the Center was not, in the strict sense of the word, a business. It is a service organization, but here again the practices and policies of the business community were required for this service to succeed.

As far as the risks were concerned, when Weinstein described what she was doing she was equally straightforward. In fact, she had some difficulty describing the project as a risk. To her way of thinking, the risk would have been to do nothing, for without embarking on this project the Center would have gone out of business, and as she knew she was providing materials that the specifically defined customer base required, this was a prospect she could not tolerate.

It is all part of an information services management picture that Robert Hayes (1993) has called 'strategic management'. It goes beyond strategic planning, Hayes writes, and although he is writing specifically about academic librarianship, the concept applies throughout the information services spectrum. In much of information services,

> ... planning cannot keep pace with developments as they actually occur. ... Rather than planning, we must concern ourselves with strategic *management*, within which planning may play a role, but at most, only a supporting one ... *Strategic management* is that part of the general management of

organizations that emphasizes the relationships to external environments, evaluates the current status and the effects of future changes in them, and determines the most appropriate organizational response. (Hayes, pp. x, 3)

This definition could have been written with Lois Weinstein and the UCMP ONline Project in mind, for what she did there was to incorporate into the general management of the organization an emphasis on the relationship with the external environment, in this case specifically MLCNY's customers and the participants in the UCMP catalog, and to determine, from an evaluation of the current state of affairs (that is, it was not well enough organized for the benefit of most of the customers), the effects of future changes (that is, the customers would stop subscribing to the database) and the most appropriate organizational response to those environments (to create a more responsive online database). In other words, to devise a product that would meet those customers' and participants' needs, and to do it in such a way that the organization as a whole could continue the synergistic role it had been playing in the medical libraries community.

On the grandest of scales, however, in terms of information services, the best example of combined strategic management and entrepreneurial thinking has taken place in another part of New York City. In this last decade of the twentieth century, the New York Public Library Research Libraries has created what might easily be characterized as a state-of-the-art specialized library, the Science, Industry and Business Library. Envisaged to be the largest public information center in the world devoted solely to science and business, and with the goal of serving an international as well as a local constituency, this information megacenter has been realized through a team of NYPL and external experts all guided by William D. Walker (who, in a curious coincidence for our purposes, had come to NYPL from the directorship of the Medical Library Center of New York). As an example of an information delivery agency that relates to (and is reacting to) the external environment, the entire creation and organization of this $100 million effort is looked upon as something of a miracle. Despite its grandeur, however, the development of this project is an event that reflects what is happening in the world of information delivery, and its very existence is built on the innovation, risk-taking, and visionary thinking that characterize entrepreneurial management.

For example, the collections and services of NYPL's SIBL (as it is affectionately called) are unusual by previous library standards, but not in terms of the needs of information seekers in the twenty-first century. In fact, Walker has pointed out that SIBL is a new model of library service, because it represents a complete rethinking of the business that the New York Public Library Research Libraries is in. The goal, according to Walker, has been to incorporate information technology, both existing and future,

into one program. This will be a library and information services operation totally unlike anything that has ever gone before. The innovation is
obvious.

The risks, of course, are monumental, and with such financial obligations in place there is no illusion that the creation and operation of
SIBL are the traditionally 'calculated' risks with which librarians and other
information services workers are assumed to be comfortable. The task
has been compared to the kind of organization and logistics that go into
building something like the tunnel under the English Channel, or a new
skyscraper, and it has been an almost superhuman effort. While such
organization, logistics and grandiose planning are commonplace and
expected in the building of, say, a tunnel or a skyscraper, they are highly
unusual in the library and information services profession, where most
'building' is based on something that already exists. What has taken place
with SIBL is a risk situation in which, once the decision had been taken,
it was 'full steam ahead'. The commitment was there, the enthusiasm and
support of the community were there, and the vision was there. There
was nothing left to do but to get on with the project, and that's what
Walker and his team did.

SIBL works because – connecting directly into Hayes' concept of
strategic management, and linking that to the very basics of entrepreneurial management – the members of New York's social, political and
financial community (and Walker and his superiors) recognized that the
information customers of the future would have needs that would tran-
scend the abilities of the current information establishment to meet. They
came together to realize a vision of information services for the scientific, business and industrial community that would meet the needs of
the customers, even when they could not predict what those needs would
be. In this case, the risk was too obvious not to take, and, as with the
Medical Library Center of New York, the real risk would have been to
do nothing.

References

Cottam, Keith M. 'Professional Identity and 'Intrapreneurial' Behavior.' *Journal of
Library Administration*, 8 (1) Spring, 1987.

Drucker, Peter F. *Innovation and Entrepreneurship: Practice and Principles*. New York:
Harper & Row, 1985.

Drucker, Peter F. *Managing the Nonprofit Organization: Principles and Practices*. New
York: HarperCollins, 1990.

Ferriero, David S. and Wilding, T.L. 'Scanning the Environment in Strategic Planning.'
Masterminding Tomorrow's Information – Creative Strategies for the '90s.
Washington, DC: Special Libraries Association, 1991.

Hayes, Robert M. *Strategic management for academic libraries*. Westport, CT:
Greenwood Press, 1993.

Chapter Three
The entrepreneurial advantage in information services

It is easy to assert that an information operation should be entrepreneurial in focus. Whether it is a library, a records management unit, a management information systems department, or any of the other numerous services that are connected with the provision of information, most managers would be inclined to agree that entrepreneurial thinking is a good thing. The next question to ask is: Why? What are the advantages that an entrepreneurial ambience brings to an organization, and particularly to the information services unit that has been created to save it?

Reference was earlier made to librarians and other information services practitioners who have a strong desire to 'stretch' themselves, to move beyond the ordinary or the commonplace and to position themselves for contributing to the achieved success of their organization or community. They are the people who test limits and create new possibilities, in Rosabeth Moss Kanter's now classic phrase, 'by pushing and directing the innovation process'. (Kanter, p. 210) What these people are doing is recognizing that change is constant in today's society (and in the workplace), and in doing so they are also recognizing that it is innovation and its incorporation into the management process that will enable their information services operations – and their organizations and communities – to participate effectively in change. That, in effect, is what entrepreneurial management brings to the workplace; entrepreneurial management permits a useful and workable framework for implementing change and the change management process, and it does so by focusing performance efforts on customers, on service, and on organizational success.

However, for entrepreneurial management to be successful it is necessary to commit the entire department or unit to an entrepreneurial perspective, which means that traditional ideas about libraries and information services might have to be replaced with an approach that incorporates a 'different' way of doing things. It might mean, in fact, throwing out collections, services and products that are no longer required and offering instead ones that users are asking for. But whether the idea is to replace an existing operation with a new service, or simply to devise new and more user-friendly ways of providing traditional services, the approach must be innovative. It must also ask, 'Why are we doing things this way?' 'Is there a *better* way of doing this?' It isn't an easy transition for libraries, as Hannelore B. Rader (1989) has noted:

> Libraries are in the center of the changes caused by the move to an information society and are certainly one of its most important components. At the core of the libraries' mission is the collection and retrieval of information for education, industry, and other needs of a democratic society. It is, therefore, imperative that libraries rise to the challenge of addressing how they will fit into the information society. Now that information has become a major commodity and the basis for most operations and decision making, entrepreneurs will surely begin to take over information delivery services as a business endeavor. Such operations will be efficient, effective, timely, appropriately packaged, and most assuredly, expensive. What effect will such operations have on libraries? (Rader, p. 161)

In fact, she answers her own question, for the role of entrepreneurial management in an information services operation is to devise and implement 'efficient, effective, timely, appropriately packaged' information services and programs, and if they are going to be 'most assuredly' expensive, it is also the obligation of the innovative entrepreneurial information services manager to devise ways of paying for them. It is not unusual today to find a fee-for-service or charge-back system in place, and while these are most typically attached to what are commonly referred to as 'value-added' services and products, the very fact that there are now avenues beyond the traditional allocations for library and information services for financing such programs is worth noting (as demonstrated, for example, in Mark Merrifield's activities in York, Pennsylvania, described in Chapter One, or those of Lois Weinstein in New York). The time has come to accept that some forms of information delivery can be fully or partially self-supporting, and that in itself is a departure from the traditional approach of a generation or two ago.

So the purpose of entrepreneurial management is to establish a framework for dealing with change. According to Donald E. Riggs (1989), it is not vision alone, however, which brings about entrepreneurial success. Riggs writes:

> Going beyond the minimum level and visualizing the steps from idea to actualization is one of the capabilities of the entrepreneur. Vision and action have to be combined in order to make things happen. (Riggs, p. 73)

The combination comes about, of course, when the entrepreneurial manager is able – and prepared – to recognize that the vision and the action are complementary. James H. May, Dean of Information Resources and Technology at California State University, Monterey Bay, discovered that it was his entrepreneurial thinking that had enabled him to structure the combined paper-based/electronic information environment that he put in place when the university's new campus was being created (Bennett, p. 6). Despite aggressively dramatic press treatment (described in the next chapter) that seemed to position the new university as a totally electronic and bookless environment, May was politely reassuring as he explained to anxious educators and prospective students that the campus would, indeed, offer students the opportunity to study from traditional sources if that was what they needed. Like Walker at SIBL, May designed his information delivery program to be one which wasn't built on formats or market segmentation: all of the students and faculty were going to need information and information products, at different levels and in different formats and, hopefully, as seamlessly as possible. What May did was to consider what they needed and then, when action was required, take the kind of action that meant that all information needs would be met. It many cases that would be through electronic delivery, but when it wasn't, the needs were just as valid and required just as much attention, and they received it.

Creating a risk-taking ambience for information employees

There is a fine line between what is commonly referred to as 'calculated' risk and foolhardiness, and it is the responsibility of the information services manager to set guidelines for the staff so that risk is incorporated into the departmental culture. At the same time, however, steps must be taken to ensure that that risk does not imperil the department's success in achieving its fundamental mission, i.e. the delivery of information services and products to its customers. What information services managers do, in effect, is create an ambience in which calculated risk is encouraged, and in which staff members understand and recognize the differences between calculated risk and mere adventurousness.

For most of us, calculated risk is something akin to establishing that 'worst-case' scenario we speak about so often: 'If I do this what is the worst that can happen? If that happens, can I live with it?' In the information services environment, such questioning leads the way to establishing the perimeters within which we can operate, the levels of risk that are acceptable in the management of this or that particular function. If, for example, the periodicals librarian is considering changing from subscription agency 'A' to subscription agency 'B,' as that librarian's manager I am obliged to ask him to determine what the risks are before proceeding. While subscription agency 'B' may very well offer an attractive delivery and billing package, are there compelling reasons for staying with subscription agency 'A'? The current agency permits claims for missing or unreceived issues within an unlimited time frame, which is very handy for those libraries which bind periodicals but for whom the binding period is often after a volume closes, meaning that for a monthly periodical the staff preparing the issues for binding might not notice that a claim is required until some months later. If subscription agency 'B' limits claims to sixty or ninety days, the periodicals librarian will be required to purchase missing issues from the publisher, often at substantial cost and thus affecting the periodicals budget unnecessarily. Obviously in this day and age, as more and more libraries move to electronic acquisition and storage for periodicals materials, such an example is not necessarily the best one to use, but it proves the point: even in a process as seemingly uncomplicated as choosing a subscription agency, risk must be considered.

In this particular case it really shouldn't be necessary for the periodicals librarian to approach the information services manager if an ambience for risk-taking has been established in the organization. If, for example, the periodicals librarian understands that he is authorized to negotiate for the library, he can visit several different subscription agency representatives (at a conference/exhibition, perhaps) and, when he finds one he likes, if he is not comfortable with the claims policy he can negotiate the policy he requires. If this calls for a slightly higher agency fee, so be it, for as one who is authorized to take risks he understands that the agreement he has negotiated will, in the long run and taking into account the other advantages over the current agency, be less expensive for his organization. The risk is worth taking and it is, after all, a calculated risk because the worst-case scenario – i.e. that agency 'B' would not provide as good a service as that currently being provided by agency 'A' – is diminished by the continued availability of agency 'A'.

How an employee reacts to the opportunity to make such decisions depends on the level of creativity and independence that has been encouraged by the manager and, having such an atmosphere in place, where the employees are trained in and understand the acceptable levels of independent decision making that operate in the organization, is one of the basic guidelines of quality customer service. Interestingly, such independence of action is an important component in such evaluative programs as Total Quality Management, quality circles and the like. The above example certainly relates to this, as the periodicals librarian is simply attempting to organize and implement a procedure which gets the bound materials to the users more effectively. The distance between the decision about which subscription agency to work with and the library's ultimate customer is, however, large, so the situation must be 'stretched' a bit to work. A clearer example is one which is frequently cited nowadays, especially as information services departments attempt to provide services to customers at remote sites. When, say, the reference librarian at a teaching hospital has found a list of citations on a particular subject that one of the staff at the hospital's burns unit, in another city, has requested, and has spoken with that person and faxed the list of citations, the customer will in all likelihood fax or call back with specific titles that she wants to see. At this point, the librarian can offer to send the materials through the hospital's in-house delivery system. However, this may require more time than the staff member at the burns unit has, in which case the librarian – if she has been given to understand that the information unit operates with such flexibility – can offer to send the material overnight, using a commercial delivery service. In many libraries such an offer is out of the question, for the 'frontline' staff simply do not have the authority to spend money on such value-added services. On the other hand, where speed of delivery is a major selling point in the quality of the service provided by the library, such services should be built in. What the service manager must do, however, is ensure that the frontline staff understand the costs involved by seeing that they are trained to determine which queries and which customers merit this service. Such a level of service delivery will require negotiating skills and evaluative processes that are not standard practice in many libraries and information centers, but if the organization is going to offer such value-added services, the effort involved in teaching the employees these skills is a necessary part of the managerial approach.

As these examples illustrate, establishing an entrepreneurial and risk-taking ambience within the organization is what leads to higher levels of quality service provision. Such an atmosphere is, in fact, an especially appropriate management technique in this day and age of employee 'liberation.' Tom Peters (1994) has already looked at these issues with respect to the business community at large, and it only remains for us to interpret his ideas on the subject into the information services community:

> With a bit of imagination, the average job – actually every job – can become an entrepreneurial challenge . . . all [entrepreneurs],
>
> execute mostly self-initiated projects.
>
> perform ad hoc problem-solving directly for individual internal or external customers.
>
> work in multifunctional configurations, with self-initiated access to experts inside and outside the company, and
>
> measure themselves on bottom-line results, based mainly on customer and teammate evaluations rather than a boss's subjective judgment. (Peters, p. 73)

Let's look at how Peters' four ideas about the entrepreneurial challenge might be applied in a library, or a records management department or an organizational archive unit. In the first place, except for those queries that come from the customer (who, of course, is initiating the interaction themselves), most of the work of a professional information services provider is self-initiated. And even when the query comes from another person, the thinking that provides the move toward the solution is self-initiated, for the information employee has specific skills and procedures at hand which will be called upon to reach the desired goal.

When the activity is internal, that is, not necessarily in response to a customer query, the self-initiation is even more necessary, for all 'back-stage' activities in an information center – the decisions about which databases to subscribe to, or how to deal with excess unsolicited materials, or considering which criteria to use for the retention of certain documents – are self-initiated. What the employee's manager must do is to establish a workplace in which such behavior is appropriate and, indeed, even required for the successful achievement of the departmental mission.

As for ad hoc problem solving, this is precisely what an information services professional does. Whether the problem is external, that is, brought to the library by a customer from elsewhere, or internal, the employee puts himself or herself to work to address that problem. Likewise, when the problem is of an administrative or organizational nature (what to do about telecommunications costs relating to information delivery, say, or how to determine which of a full set of documents pertaining to a particular project are to be retained and which are to be archived and/or discarded), the employee assumes an entrepreneurial challenge and addresses that specific problem specifically as it has been presented.

An ability to work in multifunctional configurations practically defines the information provision role, for the underlying premise behind every information delivery activity is (or should be): 'Find the information product or service this customer is requesting – *it doesn't matter where it is.*' Obviously there are all kinds of qualifications for such an 'idealized' process, but in fact, at the heart of every information interaction is the understanding (the assumption?) on the part of the customer that this is the approach that will be taken. Certainly the information provider thinks in these terms. There are limitations, of course, and barriers such as organizational bureaucracy, resource restrictions, or even departmental or organizational policy can interfere with the 'ideal' information interaction, but it should be recognized that, in most people's minds, this is the standard that is expected.

The information professional is thus quite comfortable moving about in the multifunctional configurations open to him in his particular workplace. The employees of the marketing information center at a major manufacturing plant are quite comfortable about going to the corporate library if a customer's needs are more effectively met through the resources of that library, just as they will comfortably approach the staff in the R&D technical library if the materials and information required are to be found there. In fact, the establishment of information 'kiosks' located at various strategic positions throughout the site, each staffed with a single employee who is skilled at information referral, has become an information delivery goal in many organizations. The customers want what they call 'one-stop shopping', and an information expert who can go to the appropriate resource for the information and deliver it to the customer is a far superior service, from the point of view of the customer, than an arrangement where the customer themselves must decide where to go.

Finally, entrepreneurial information employees measure themselves and their success according to results, and it is here that the information inter-action comes back to the taking of risks. In a unit which exists to supply information to an established customer base, the bottom line is seldom profit or financial gain: it is the satisfaction of the customer with the information product, service or consultation that is delivered as a result of the query. The risk is not calculated at all: it is simply one of providing

Figure 3.1

the service or not providing it. The measure is simple: is the customer satisfied? When an customer calls an information provider with a request, it is critical that the person taking the call be able to understand the question, know the level of service the customer expects, and be able to provide the products or services at that level. Otherwise, the 'bottom-line results', as Peters calls them, will not measure up (Figure 3.1).

Take, for example, a situation in which the information center in a public relations firm provides what it calls a 'full-service' information provision program. The center advertises its services in these terms, and as the established customer base includes both internal staff and clients of the firm through certain contractual arrangements, the expectations of all who hear about the information center are very high. However, there are days when the information staff are very busy, and not enough attention is always given to the information interview. In one such interaction, the client, not having used the center before but having been exposed to the sophisticated and high-class marketing materials sent out, called and asked for information about crisis management, a not-uncommon request in the public relations field. The information center has often had requests about this subject, and there is a standard list of citations on file. As is often the case in a busy information center, the employee who took the call had a number of other activities distracting him at the time, and so he simply replied that he would send the customer some material; out went the list of citations. However, if the employee had taken the time to turn the query into a proper information interview, he would have known that the customer wanted information about crisis management, not information about where to get information. As a result, this client received less than full service: the information interaction had failed.

How the pro-risk manager operates

There are a number of specific, proactive steps the information services manager can take to ensure that staff members are comfortable working as entrepreneurs. Five of these can be identified.

Hire people who will take risks

The staff of the information services unit must understand that the unit's role is entrepreneurial, and that it is the duty and obligation of each employee to look for opportunities which can lead to progressively better and fuller services for the identified client base. So a first look at the risk-taking characteristics of employees working in (or being considered for work in) the department recognizes that the characteristics of success in entrepreneurial management as it connects with information services are not negative. Much has been written about how difficult entrepreneurs are to get along with, about their stubbornness, their selfishness, their insensitivity. Indeed, for many people, the concept of service embodied in librarianship contrasts so strongly with the arrogance commonly attached to the entrepreneurial personality that they have difficulty accepting that the link can be made.

What is proposed here is an entirely different perspective, and that is that we can look at the beneficial aspects of entrepreneurial activity that are practiced – or meant to be practiced – in librarianship and apply them to information services as a whole. In this context, risk-taking is not a negative virtue but is the very foundation upon which customer-focused information services are built.

What are these positive attributes and how do they connect with librarianship? And how do we seek them out in our employees? And as part of the effort to move in an entrepreneurial direction, can these characteristics be further connected with information services at large? Keith Cottam (1987) has identified a long list of characteristics which he summed up as 'individuality, determination, persistence, vision for new ideas and opportunities, flexibility and a willingness to take calculated risks'. Certainly these might be called the 'highlights', but his longer list provides a more useful point of departure for a discussion of the entrepreneurial characteristics to be sought in staff employed to work in the information environment. Cottam's position requires that these employees be self-assured and self-reliant, that they have a clear professional identity and clarity of purpose in their role, both in the information department and in the employing organization. They must, of course, have trust in their colleagues and be willing to commit to collaborative relationships, but they also must be able to work autonomously and have the ability to stand on their own in meeting the responsibilities connected with their work. Above all, they must have what Cottam calls an 'aptitude for initiative', which means that they must have imagination, they must be able to think critically, and they must be visionary about their department, their organization, and about the information services profession in general. Naturally, they must be industrious, productive, honest and upright and, as much as anything else, be willing to be accountable for the work they do (Cottam, pp. 28–29).

Much of this approach to staff qualifications has to do with the employee's feelings about himself, and in this respect one could do worse than Cottam has done in turning to Gail Sheehy's famous (1981) book, *Pathfinders*, and look for people who have 'a positive self-concept reflecting a person's ability to trust others, to be confident in assuming responsibilities and to direct initiative toward changing the self and the environment'. Also looked for, according to the Sheehy/Cottam model, is '. . . a sense of right timing [and] . . . an ability to anticipate present needs as well as to prepare for the future' (Sheehy, quoted in Cottam, pp. 31).

What we have, then, is an approach to staff requirements and staff development that requires that managers take an almost personal interest in the entrepreneurial qualities that staff display, and work with them in order to enhance those qualities for the workplace. The success of the information services unit is so bound up in the risk-taking and entre-preneurial dimensions of staff work that to neglect or 'downplay' the value of these qualities is to jeopardize the success the department expects to achieve: without staff who think entrepreneurially, the information services unit will not succeed, at least not at the levels at which it could succeed if its employees saw themselves as risk-takers and entrepreneurs.

Train (and evaluate) staff for their entrepreneurial skills

These thoughts lead to a second consideration for the information services manager, and that is that staff be given the opportunity to be trained and evaluated not simply in terms of their information-delivery tasks, but in management concepts that relate to the successful realization of those tasks. If, for example, a staff member is uncomfortable making presentations and yet the information services manager has determined that departmental presentations are an essential part of the unit's marketing program, it behoves that manager to encourage the employee to attend seminars and workshops on presentation methods. If the employee balks, it must be explained that the work of the information service unit is not limited to simply waiting for customers to come in, but includes such proactive efforts as departmental presentations as well (Figure 3.2).

Managers of information services operations must make special efforts to find people who are comfortable in an entrepreneurial environment and with such an approach to their work. In Melbourne, Australia, Meg Paul takes quite seriously her role as an adviser and consultant to Australia's library community, and one of her guiding principles is the recognition that a quality service ethos – as she refers to it – is set and owned by the library or information operation's staff. Although the end result is better service, the approach is not totally altruistic for staff members learn that by participating in the establishment of a quality service they themselves benefit, with more fulfilling employment, better interpersonal relations and the winning of approval from the organiza-tion or community.

Catherine A. Jones, Chief of the Congressional Reference Division at the Library of Congress, Washington DC, has worked hard to establish a similar entrepreneurial environment, and it is one in which the staff is highly motivated to perform for the benefit of the customers, in this case members and staff of the United States Congress. The approach that Jones and her senior staff have taken is one that, as she puts it, respects the integrity of the individual: everything that can be done to help the

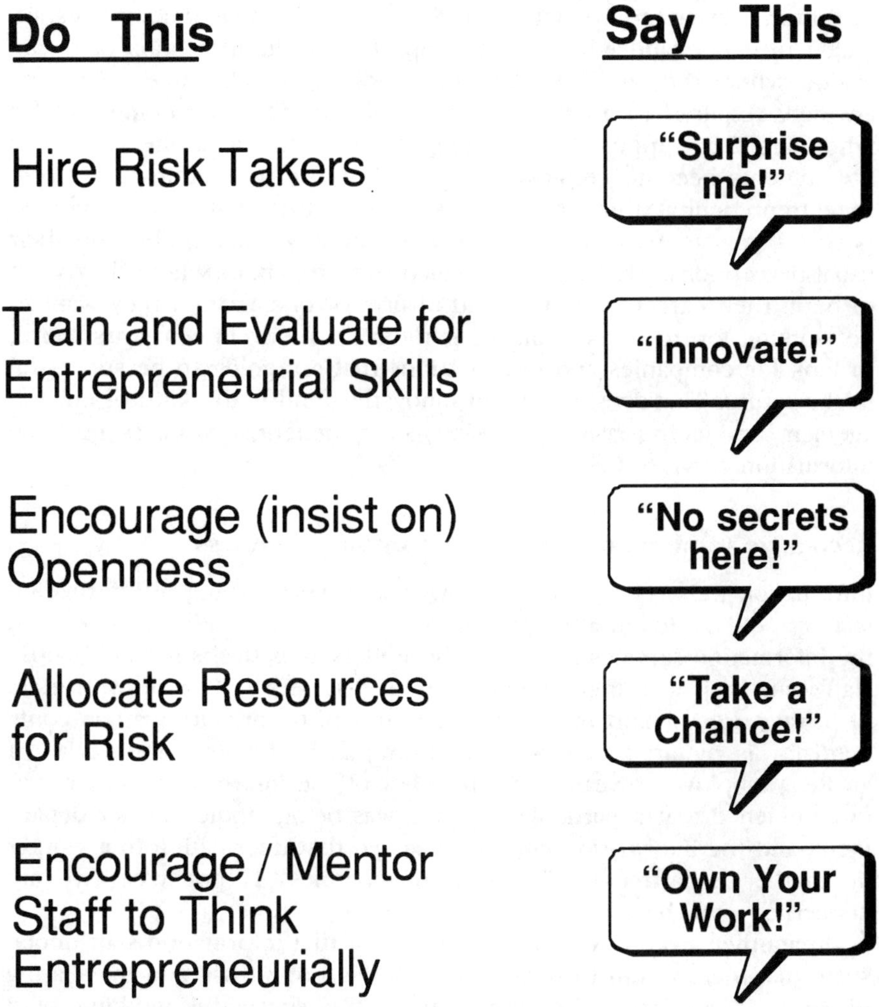

Do This

Say This

Hire Risk Takers

"Surprise me!"

Train and Evaluate for Entrepreneurial Skills

"Innovate!"

Encourage (insist on) Openness

"No secrets here!"

Allocate Resources for Risk

"Take a Chance!"

Encourage / Mentor Staff to Think Entrepreneurially

"Own Your Work!"

Figure 3.2   Pro-risk management

employees do their best is done. For example, jobs are codified as much as they can be, and managers and supervisors are careful to tell their people just what is expected of them. It relates back to an old managerial adage, that the best way to succeed in management is to hire the best people, tell them what to do, and let them do it. When employees are shown that they are respected and that they are *trusted* to perform at their best for the benefit of their customers, they will do what they are supposed to do.

It's a concept that is beginning to creep into the training of information professionals, and James Matarazzo, Dean and Professor at the Graduate School of Library and Information Science at Simmons College in Boston, Massachusetts, takes special care to see that the students are taught to understand what is really important in the institution or organization where they will be working. According to Matarazzo, librarians are now required to ask what they are supposed to be doing and for whom are they supposed to be doing it. When this idea filters down as the students become employees, they will be in a position to perform as entrepreneurial thinkers, to look at jobs that will – as Matarazzo puts it – reward them in different ways, in ways that go beyond their usual perceptions. They are encouraged to think about where they want to be in their careers, and the kind of firm or organization they want to be working for; to think about their futures, to look fifteen years ahead; to look for companies and organizations that are going to be successful in the future. That's visionary and innovative, and is the kind of encouragement and enthusiasm that brings entrepreneurial workers into the information services field.

Recognize (and encourage – insist upon) openness

Information today is regarded as power, and the hoarding of information is a very old-fashioned attempt at control. It doesn't work any more, and the information services manager who understands this is the one whose staff value their working relationship with that person. Obviously, matters of privacy are not part of this, and certainly in proprietary matters confidentiality is required. It would, for example, be highly inappropriate if an R&D employee revealed to a member of the information center staff in confidence that a particular process was being studied in her department, and the information employee passed that information to a worker in another department. This kind of openness is not what we are concerned with here.

On another level, however, it is important that information staff understand that the unit must operate as a team and that trust, and the sharing of trust, is an essential component in the successful working of a team. The idea of assigning work to an employee with the comment 'Just do it – don't ask any questions' is rude and insulting and puts the employee in a very awkward position, simply because questions might be required for the success of the project. Similarly, while a customer might request confidentiality on a query, if the person who receives the query is going to bring others into the process of tracing the information the customer is seeking, it is inappropriate to ask them to help without telling them, in confidence, the full story of the request. In bank libraries, for example, it is quite common for those seeking information about a particular client or proposed deal to require confidentiality, but those who are called in to work on the assignment can be expected, if they are professionals and understand their role, to respect the confidence of those seeking the information.

The same openness is required in relation to the fiscal operations of the information services department. There are those managers who feel that it is none of the staff's business how the departmental funds are allocated and apportioned, but, for successful management it is important that all staff understand the financial implications of their work. The fact that an online service's subscription budget exceeds the processing team's budget for outsourced cataloging services for the company's technical reports is not relevant to the work being produced, or to the eventual delivery of the products to the customers. But by sharing information, each member of the team is sent the message that he *really* is part of the team, that his opinions are worth having, and that he is valued as much for his overall knowledge of the workings of the department as for his particular special interest.

Allocate resources for (calculated) risk

Related to this is the manner in which funds and other resources, including staff, are allocated for the achievement of the department's goals. All information services workers are now aware that while in some institutions 'There is no more money', there is money in other departments that can be requisitioned for information services if a case can be made that such money will add to organizational success. Similarly within the department itself some divisions or sections might be operating for the wrong reasons, and it is important that there be an openness about the department's finances so that all staff understand what the financial arrangement is and feel free to question the value of this or that service or product. In the library of a historical society, for example, the preservation and cataloging of late 19th-century photographs became a priority a few years ago, and with the benefit of special grants and a handsome endowment procured for the purpose, a strong historic photographs section was created. Now the organization's emphasis has shifted to scanning and digitizing the contents of the manuscripts collection, and funds are being organized for that activity. Thus the grants program has shifted from the photograph project (which continues to receive income from the endowment fund for its support) to manuscripts, but for the library staff to function as a team, and for the services to continue at the level to which the employees have become accustomed, it is necessary that all staff understand what the financial picture is. Such openness leads to a healthier and more entrepreneurial ambience for the organization as a whole.

A related condition has to do with the 'mood' of the organization in its relations with information staff. If the prevailing mood is one in which the parent organization appears to be cheap (as opposed to financially prudent), the staff are not going to be willing to take risks and the entrepreneurial thrust of the information unit is not going to lead to anything.

Two examples can demonstrate this. In a major art museum in New York City, a private museum which had recently developed serious financial difficulties, the highly entrepreneurial staff of the research library were suddenly confronted with a crisis. Having over the years built up a thriving business in the organization, development and marketing of specific information products relating to the exhibitions frequently put on at the museum, the information staff was producing annual revenues of nearly a hundred thousand dollars, in addition to providing standard information services and products for the museum's curatorial staff, the academic art community in the metropolitan area, and, upon request and the payment of a research fee, the general public. With its financial crisis, the museum's administrators looked at operations and decided that library services could go. 'After all,' one of them said publicly, 'we can get the books we need from other museum libraries, through interlibrary loan, and we just won't have any other library services.'

Unfortunately, the idea backfired, for as the library staff were dismissed, except for one person to 'run the library' and an assistant to be in charge of the revenue-generating activities, word spread through the library community. Suddenly, interlibrary loans were no longer available for this library; worse yet, the person in charge of the income-producing side of the program lost all enthusiasm, her entrepreneurial interest waned and eventually was lost altogether, and the library, through a pattern of desuetude and neglect, was doomed. Had the museum's administrators understood the asset they had in the enthusiastic, entrepreneurially thinking staff in the first place, they would have taken advantage of it and come to some success, instead of the reverse.

A second example has to do with an information services company which was purchased by another, much larger, company. The merger had seemed a good idea to many people in the information services community but, in fact, there were problems almost from the beginning, primarily because the company which was purchased had operated from an enthusiastically entrepreneurial point of view throughout its history and the new company, which was early on characterized as 'cheap' by its new employees, almost immediately after the purchase instituted budget structures that effectively eliminated any entrepreneurial activities on the part of the staff. The mood of the company changed from proactive to reactive, and the sad end of the story was not hard to predict: the sales force lost its enthusiasm, the customers began to realize that they could get similar services and products from other suppliers, and the business suffered. It did not have to happen, but it did because the staff discovered that it could not support a company that was anti-entrepreneurial in its approach to business.

Encourage and mentor staff to think entrepreneurially

If information services managers want to get the best from their employees, they must learn to recognize that not all people work well in highly structured, rigid environments, and even though some structure is required, when possible employees should be encouraged to think about their work and seek out entrepreneurial and risk-taking occasions for the department. Brian Champion (1988) has looked at this concept in library management, and among his conclusions is one that is particularly germane here: that all these employees need is 'freedom to think and create, a little money to help bring some of their ideas to life, and institutional support'. When these are in place, Champion suggests, they lead to 'the bestowal of the best reward of all, credit and recognition' (Champion, p. 37).

Management literature already includes many suggestions as to how these employees can be so encouraged, and for many information services managers all that is required is a slight change in attitude within the framework of the job. For example, while sabbaticals are not quite the norm in the public library community, or the corporate world in which specialized libraries and information centers are found, information employees serving these sorts of institutions can in fact be awarded 'planning' time by linking time off or release time to attendance at professional conferences, continuing education and professional development programs. Sending an employee responsible for supervising and training the online search staff to a three-day marketing program at one of the vendors, and then encouraging that employee to take an extra two or three days to visit some of the vendor's other clients before returning to work, will produce useful, tangible results. In fact, his arrival back at the office will be accompanied by such a conglomeration of entrepreneurial, proactive ideas that the staff who work with him (and his manager) might begin to wish he had never gone! At the same time, however, as he sorts through the ideas and talks them over, it will become apparent that there are ways in which the services the information unit offers can be better offered and marketed to the customers. What has happened is that the employee, given the opportunity to see beyond the parent organization's immediate needs, can begin to visualize the kind of services that *could* be offered, and that is where true entrepreneurialism begins.

Champion goes so far as to suggest that, in encouraging staff to be more creative and entrepreneurial, managers would do well to use a formula not usually associated with the information services. 'The five-to-fifteen rule,' Champion writes, 'ought to be applied to librarians: 5 to 15% of the professional staff time should be slotted for the pursuit of ideas in a wide spectrum of interests (2–5 hours a week in a 37.5 hour week)' (Champion, p. 41). For many information services managers, especially in the corporate world, such time allocations are an unrealized luxury, and in any case much of the corporate world, especially in those areas where entrepreneurial thinking is expected and encouraged, does not adhere to specific work weeks. Nowadays, the achievers and others who excel in the workplace put themselves on a much longer work week than 37.5 or 40 hours – indeed, in many organizations they are *expected* to do so – but they nevertheless need this time to think. It is an important part of the successful delivery of any service, but in information services, especially today with so many new products and services coming on the market all the time, such 'planning' time is almost a requirement for success. The wise information services manager recognizes this, and does all she can to see that her staff has every possible opportunity to have this time.

This is not to say that there are not problems associated with this type of activity. Of course such encouragement can lead to problems with the organization of the work, and there will be times when the encouragement of such enthusiasm has to be controlled. In the long run, however, the rewards are worth the effort, for the working of the information services section will be better, of a higher level, and, certainly more customer oriented, which is the ultimate goal.

Finally, it is useful to take a look at an idea that Stan Davis and Bill Davidson put forward in their 1992 book about business transformation. Libraries and similar information-related operations are not usually part of the profit-making 'mainstream'. Nevertheless, when it is accepted that their products and services contribute to the achievement of organizational success, there are still ways to apply in an information services construct the idea that Davis and Davidson recommend. Their idea, which they refer to as 'A new design limit: each employee equals a business', is this:

> Make employees into entrepreneurs who have legal and economic owner-
> ship of the business for which they are responsible. When the model focuses
> on the businesses, that is, the customer in the marketplace, the way to gain
> importance is through profitable customer service. When the focus shifts
> from organization to business, internal 'customers' become real customers,
> and the level of service improves.
>   The social consequences of such an economic organization would be
> democratizing. Traditionally, the people who perform service jobs have always
> been given a lower status. Staff is to corporations what domestics are to a
> wealthy family. The place may not be run without them, but they are not
> the ones the place runs for. (Davis and Davidson, p. 46)

If this concept is moved to the information services environment radical changes are required, but when information services managers can work with their staffs to teach them how to focus on the business at hand – the effective and efficient delivery of information products and services to the customers – when they are given 'ownership' of the services they provide, the customer becomes the focus and the delivery of the products the customers want (not what the staff thinks the customers should have) becomes the object. It works in business, and it can work in information services.

References

Bennett, Lettie. 'The Real Story Behind the New 'Library-Less Campus'.' *InfoManage: The International Management Newsletter for the Information Services Executive*, 2 (6), May, 1995.

Champion, Brian. 'Intrapreneuring and the Spirit of Innovation in Libraries.' *Journal of Library Administration*, 9 (2), 1988.

Cottam, Keith M. 'Professional Identity and 'Intrapreneurial' Behavior.' *Journal of Library Administration*, 8 (1), Spring, 1987.

Davis, Stan and Davidson, Bill *2020 Vision: Transform Your Business Today to Succeed in Tomorrow's Economy*. New York: Simon and Schuster, 1992.

Kanter, Rosabeth Moss. *The Change Masters*. New York: Simon & Schuster, 1983.

Peters, Tom. *The Tom Peters Seminar: Crazy Times Call for Crazy Organizations*. New York: Vintage Press, 1994.

Rader, Hannelore B. 'Teamwork and entrepreneurship.' *Journal of Library Administration*, 10 (2/3), 1989.

Riggs, Donald E. 'Making Creative, Innovative, and Entrepreneurial Things Happen in the Special Library.' *Journal of Library Administration*, 10 (2/3), 1989.

Sheehy, Gail. *Pathfinders*. New York: William Morrow and Company, 1981.

Chapter Four

'The shifting paradigms'

In all enterprises, responsive service has become the standard criterion for measuring success. As information services managers seek ever newer ways to motivate staff there is increased attention being given to patterns, models and paradigms. Managers want to know how other managers do it, what techniques and methodologies they employ to achieve their success. Much of the general management literature of recent years has put heavy emphasis on the concepts of paradigms, models and the like, and popular management thinkers (Joel Barker, for example, and Rosabeth Moss Kanter) find themselves giving attention to the 'shifting' of paradigms, to the idea that the models that worked for previous generations of managers aren't so sacrosanct any more, that changing and developing social forces now require managers to give attention to different details, different focuses, and, particularly, to different rewards for the people who report to them.

The information services paradigms

Entrepreneurial librarianship is about change management, and while it might be argued that those who have responsibility for libraries and other information services should be able to direct change without resorting to entrepreneurial management, it is certainly a natural and appropriate step to look to entrepreneurial librarianship as a framework for making the change process easier and (in organizational terms) more acceptable. A paradigm is classically defined as an example or pattern, a model or worthy of imitation. For example, we're thinking in paradigms when we react to a story in a news magazine such as the one that describes a major paradigm shift in academic librarianship:

> When California State University drew up plans for their newest campus, scheduled to open this fall at the old Fort Ord Site in Monterey Bay, one

building was conspicuously absent from their blueprints: the library. But as Barry Munitz, chancellor of the 22-campus system, sees it, why bother wasting all that money on bricks and mortar and expensive tomes when it could be better spent on technology for getting information via computer? 'You simply don't have to build a traditional library these days,' Munitz says. . . .

The University of Texas at Austin built a microcomputer center, equipped with 200 computers, using money from a $150-per-student computer fee. Carved into existing stacks of the undergraduate library, the $2 million center has displaced about 85,000 books. . . . (Hafner, pp. 62–63)

Depending on one's particular point of view, reaction may vary from abject horror at the elimination of the much-vaunted 'heart' of a university to total approval of the common sense displayed by the university's administration in recognizing that, for most citizens educated in the modern university the need for a library of books is as remote as their need for much else that has been eliminated from the curriculum. The paradigm – the traditional library warehouse containing everything that any student might need in the course of his or her education – has been rejected by the administrators. Instead, resources formerly allocated for traditional library purposes are now to be used for products and services that fit the needs of the students as determined by the administrators. The administrators have reacted with a classic paradigm shift: when they questioned the logic of the putting the resources into a traditional library and matched their findings against the usefulness and applicability of the paradigm formerly in place, they made a change. They asked, 'Why are we doing it that way?' and the answers were not very satisfying.

There was an even further 'paradigm shift,' for on further consideration it was discovered in the planning for the new campus that the bookless campus was not as near at hand as had been so gleefully claimed in the news media. So the shifting of paradigms can depend, in great degree, on just which paradigms are in fashion at any given moment in time.

However, it should be pointed out that paradigm shifts are not necessarily related to information technology and the move toward a different kind of information delivery in the future. Throughout the history of information services there have been managers who were concerned with paradigm shifts, but they did not necessarily refer to them in such terms. In fact, they were being what we would consider typically 'entrepreneurial', for they were looking for opportunities for better service, and when they found those opportunities they took advantage of them. It is therefore not difficult to determine that we're also thinking in paradigms when we look at a typical information delivery operation, a research library, say, at a weekly news magazine, and recognize that the usual services can be enhanced to everyone's advantage. In such a library, typical patterns of information provision on demand, the organization and preservation of specifically designated files, and the acquisition and distribution of requested materials to a defined user base within the editorial staff are the foundations on which the department is established. The paradigm shifts, however, when we determine, as Ted Slate did at *Newsweek* when he joined the staff as Library Director in 1966, (and the date establishes Slate as an original paradigm 'shifter'), that a company's library could move beyond its original service sphere. When Slate retired in 1994, the story was told about how he had been convinced, when he was hired, that the library needed to be broader in focus, and he determined to initiate an information-services thrust directed at the business side of the magazine. Slate knew that management, sales and the other financial entities at *Newsweek* required information, and he also knew that his library's staying power would have something to do with how executives on the business side perceived the library service. So Slate extended the library's services to the business staff as well, going to annual sales meetings, doing presentations, and generally offering the management side of the company an information resource it had not had before. Of course it worked, and today the support of corporate activities represents a significant proportion of the work of the library.

In simple terms, the paradigm shifted. Slate could see that at some point in the future information would become a key focus for corporate activities beyond the editorial departments his staff currently served, and he wanted his library to be there when the need was recognized. He changed the paradigm, as Paul B. Thornton (1994) has put it, in order 'to create new opportunities' (Thornton, p. 46). In changing the paradigm, however, Slate also carefully ensured that his operation was serving the people in the organization who, when they were forced to look for vulnerable services to cut back, would look elsewhere and not at the information delivery system.

Paradigms are not only about models, however, or about looking at patterns and establishing how they do or do not work and then attempting to find new models to achieve the same or better results. Several writers, including Paul Thornton, have opened up the concept of the paradigm and define it as 'an attitude, belief or viewpoint about how things should look and function' (Thornton, p. 46). The manager's ideas *about* the work become linked with his ideas about *how* to work, and as society changes so do people's ideas about what they are going to do on the job and what their expectations are from the various services and suppliers they use in order to do their work. Thus not only is the established model of a research library in a petroleum company going to become outdated and ineffective if it isn't changed to match the changing demands and requirements of the industry and of society at large, it must also develop new paradigms of service relating to the changed expectations of the people who use it and the people who staff it.

The second era of the information age

After information services managers have dealt with change management for a while, it becomes clear that those who espouse the concept that change is inevitable and desirable must ensure that their staffs themselves understand the value of change. Sylvia Piggott has achieved a certain level of prominence in the information services field for a concept she came

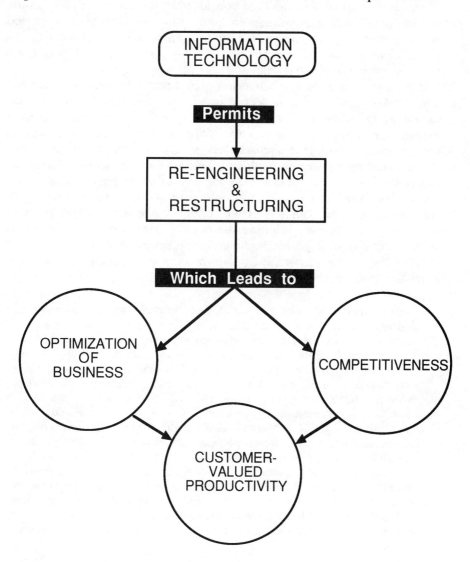

Figure 4.1   Piggott's second era of the information age

Adapted from Sylvia E.A. Piggott, February, 1995

up with over the course of the last few years, that information services as a management discipline has now gone beyond its beginning stages into a 'second era'. Because of what she characterizes as 'enabling technology' and the application of reengineering constructs to the information services field, the much talked-about information age is now moving into its second generation, so to speak. For two decades or so, the world at large – and certainly the information services management community – was impressed by and directed considerable resources towards getting 'up to speed' with the changes in information technology. That period is now over, Piggott contends, and from now on reengineering processes can be applied to information delivery just as they are fit to basic business processes ('Sylvia Piggott . . . ', pp. 1–2) (Figure 4.1).

It is all part of a major change in organizational management that has been evolving over the past decade or so, and librarians and other information services workers are wise to incorporate this change into their management programs. The essence of the change has been captured in the remarkable work that Michael Hammer and his colleagues have been doing in the reengineering field, and their advice is as applicable for the entrepreneurial library manager as for any other manager: 'Companies should ask "How can we use technology to allow us to do things that we are not already doing?" Reengineering, unlike automation, is about innovation. It is about exploiting the latest capabilities of technology to achieve entirely new goals' (Hammer and Champy, p. 85).

What Piggott and others are doing, of course, is establishing a major paradigm shift for the information services field:

> We are entering an era where businesses and professions are reengineering and restructuring as a consequence of the exponential leap in information technology. This reengineering and restructuring, some believe, will lead to vast improvements in customer-valued productivity, optimization of businesses, and competitiveness. The corporate world expects products to be delivered faster, using more flexible manufacturing and distribution processes with the ability to get products anywhere, 24 hours a day. In this kind of environment, information professionals, especially in the corporate world, must also be looking for ways to optimize their services by reengineering and restructuring. Corporate library managers, to keep in sync with this kind of performance, must reengineer their libraries or information centers to deliver information using the most cost-effective tools and products available in the industry. In addition, the library or information center must seek to exist as a borderless service, a place where information can be sought wherever it exists and used immediately by local or remote customers. Business information professionals must make the adjustment as, except in rare cases, only real time information will be valued as a competitive tool. (Piggott, p. 11)

It is this 'borderless service', this 'real time' information 'used immediately by local or remote customers' that establishes Piggott's powerful paradigm of information delivery as being so important for modern information services managers. Whether the operation is a traditional library, a specialized corporate library (of the type Piggott is specifically addressing in her work), a records department in a large organization or government entity, or even a corporate or organizational enterprise, this 'second era' is an important motivating concept for those responsible for managing the information services function. Think about, for example, the patient records section of a large metropolitan hospital, one of those huge medical centers in a major city whose buildings spread out over a wide-ranging campus of traditional hospital buildings, specialty 'wings', outpatient care facilities, research laboratories and diagnostic facilities, parking garages and the like. It is obviously not easy to transport things around the campus, and the process is cumbersome and time consuming. Even printed paper copies of library materials are moved about through this system, which is why interdepartmental fax is the second most preferred choice of delivery. The first choice, of course, is online delivery, and as patient records are digitized and available for qualified staff to access throughout the organization, the move toward digitization of library materials becomes equally attractive. The established paradigm of getting information as soon as possible gives way to the new paradigm that not only enables the staff to access either type of information in real time from a remote site, but provides the possibility that the two types of information can, when required, be linked together and accessed at the same time. The advantages for improved medical care are obvious, and with appropriate training and management support, the shift to such a new paradigm of information delivery is a much-anticipated improvement.

Key competencies

Although the successful management of information services is not predicated on an adherence to any particular paradigm recognition, it has to be accepted that in all management, the attitudes and viewpoints of those in positions of authority influence the levels of success that are achieved within the enterprise. The models that one brings to information services drastically affect how those services are structured and function, and one of the primary conflicts in information services management during the last quarter of the twentieth century has been the misunderstanding and misperceptions of senior management regarding the information function.

Part of this confusion lies in preconceived paradigms that are accepted without question (as evidenced by the lack of distinction between information and information technology, which is discussed below). There are, however, other paradigms that are shifting, and although many information services professionals understand the need for the shift, we are still, as a society, locked into a major battle with ignorance about what information providers do. It isn't necessarily a major issue in most circumstances, but in organizations that position the information services operation as a 'necessary evil', and where the information provided is perceived as being non-essential, the problem is usually one of ignorance on the part of senior management.

The problem has most often come about because the paradigm of information delivery held by those managers is inaccurate or outdated. Regardless of whether the information provided is internal, as with a records management department, or external, acquired through a library or information center, its value to managerial decision makers is connected with their use of information and how the information function is described for them. For example, in an organization where the corporate archives are the responsibility of an archives section, with duly qualified staff and a conscientious and equally qualified manager, if the company's senior management needs to refer to the archives, or if there is an information-intensive section of senior management that requires frequent interaction with the archive staff, the senior management are going to value the services of the archives section. If, on the other hand, the archives section exists solely for historical/legal reasons and none of the senior management staff has need to refer to the materials, the paradigm those people will bring to the situation will be one of past experience regarding the concept of archives, what they have heard or learned from educational experiences much earlier in their lives, and the effect of this model on the effectiveness of the archives section will be great.

There are occasions, however, when paradigms can be shifted through the efforts of the information services staff: as information services move toward the new century, among the qualifications for success in the field are an understanding of and an ability to employ aggressive and assertive techniques for changing existing paradigms. In a delightful and stimulating flight of fancy published in 1993, Stephen K. Abram described a fictionalized 'information coach' in the corporate world of 2005 (in an earlier time, she might have been known as a 'specialized librarian', or 'information manager', or 'information specialist'). Her role, as Abram described it, 'is to use her highly developed information skills to leverage decision making' at the company where she is employed. As a 'transformational librarian', she is expected to possess not only the usual skills required for information services management, she is also required to understand and implement four additional core competencies, which Abram enumerated as follows:

> *True information literacy* – Not merely technological or computer literacy, not the entry-level skill of numeracy or language literacy or just research and communication skills – but the ability to combine a deep understanding of information dynamics with advanced interpersonal and empathy skills to deliver answers that support client decision.

Selling skills – not just marketing ability. Since information was now the commodity that drove the economies of the [company], it was now essential that leaders in the information industry be completely at ease with pricing and closing the sales of information transactions.

Affiliative abilities – . . . Alliances among companies were now the norm. . . . The ability to construct on-the-fly temporary, and sometimes long-term, alliances between information industry players (including vendors, intellectual property creators, copyright owners, libraries, etc.) was essential to create the multimedia, multi-dimensional packages clients now demanded.

Strategic thinking – . . . The organization now placed much lower value on traditional managerial and supervisory skills and higher value on analytical and critical thinking skills, advanced networking and teamwork abilities, independent work styles, information handling skills, and communication skills that went beyond the 'excellent oral and written communication skills' of [her] early career. (Abram, p. 214)

Think about the impact an employee with these competencies can have in an organization, particularly where senior management is operating from a paradigm that is not only no longer appropriate for the information services function but which can hamper the success of the organization in achieving its corporate goals. For example, in the scenario described above, where the corporate archives are relegated to a position of mere tolerance or minimal value to the organization, if the archives manager aspires to succeed as a 'transformational librarian' (even though he and his staff are not strictly librarians at all), he will find ways to fit these additional core competencies into his and his staff's working qualifications, and will apply them to the successful functioning of the archives department. At the same time, by employing those competencies, he will be providing senior management with the information and value-added services they need in order to understand the role of the archives in the company's overall information services picture. In addition, he and his staff will be providing the raw material that will influence senior management in shifting their paradigms about archives from an invalid one to one that serves the needs of the corporation. How will the archives manager be able to do this? Three activities combine.

Matching information services management to organizational goals

There is never any question in an information services operation that there must be a connection between organizational and departmental goals. As a first step, the archives manager will determine the value of the archives to the corporation, why they are retained in the medium in which they are retained (e.g. hard copy, online records, CD-ROM etc.), and what kind of organizational policy there is for retention policies, off-site storage, access etc. As these issues are studied, the archives manager and his staff will be obtaining information that will require consultation with senior management about organizational policy, and the department will be required to relate its services to the goals of the company as a whole. With this information, the archive staff are then in a position to apply their work to that of the company. In other words, their place in the company is being established, rather than simply accepted because it was always there.

Matching information staff competencies with organizational needs

This is where the archives manager brings into play the 'new' core competencies that Abram recommends, in order to enhance his and his staff's role in the organization. The true information literacy that Abram calls for will be applied, not only in knowing how and in what media to acquire and store archival information, but the very presence of the archives in a digitized format will enable the staff to look for electronic enhancements. The archives manager and his staff can use their interactions with appropriate staff throughout the corporation to determine exactly what the organization needs from the archives and, with their sophisticated understanding of the information delivery process, organize and design a system that enables staff to access this information from their desks.

The selling skills that Abram calls for are used not only for determining how archival information is used throughout the company, but in determining costs, advising other departments about their share in the allocation of resources for this activity, and, of course, in the marketing and delivery of the services the customers have decided they need.

Affiliative abilities are used by the archives manager and his staff to work with suppliers, particularly with the vendors of electronic services and products, simply because the investment in any of these enhancements is significant and organization staff want the simplest and most user-friendly applications possible. An obvious choice for such affiliative activity will be the installation of a fax-on-demand system, with a dedicated direct line from every desk to the archive unit, so that by keying in a password and an ordering code the relevant document or parts thereof can be accessed. To develop such a system is relatively simple but to install it and have it supported seamlessly and without losing staff time will require an ability to build and work with alliances.

Finally, for the archives staff to contribute successfully to the achievement of organizational goals, strategic thinking is required. This means that the archives manager must be able to relate to what the company is attempting to do, to how the archives and the delivery of information affect corporate success, and how strategic planning and management within the department are linked to the strategic management that takes place throughout the company. To do this requires communication between the archives manager and various department and division managers to determine their needs, in terms of both delivering information services and products to them and determining which materials generated by their departments should be delivered to the archives. It means that retention policies and other departmental procedures cannot be rigid: they must be built on a flexible framework giving information stakeholders the maximum value in their access efforts (Figure 4.2).

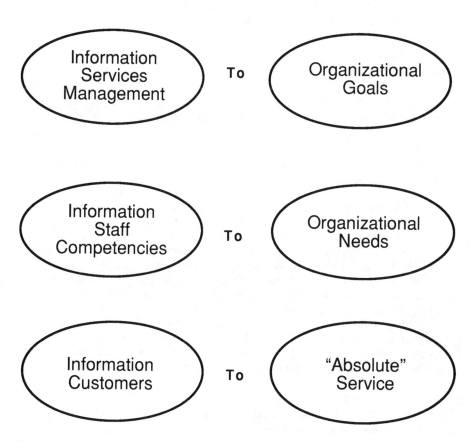

Figure 4.2   To shift the information paradigms

Matching information customers with 'absolute' service

There are no compromises in this organizational archive: if the customer does not get exactly what she has asked for, the information interaction continues until she does. And it is the customer who determines whether the interaction has been successful or not. While such a proposal might seem to be radical, it is part of the new paradigm that this company will have created as the archives manager and his staff investigate organizational needs and determine the best ways to meet them. In today's environment, if the information services operation is to succeed as a critical part of the organization it serves, customer satisfaction must be the primary driving force. This means, of course, that the archives manager and his staff will spend what might seem to be an inordinate amount of time in training activities, in the information interview, in working with the client to help him or her bring forth exactly what it is he or she is seeking. In the long run, of course, such efforts are well worth while since the criteria for success in the interaction have been mutually established by the customer and the information provider.

Information is not information technology

In a paper describing how corporate library managers might look at some of the issues that come between them and others in the organizations where they are found, Laurence Prusak identified several 'influences' that have affected how businesses view information and information management. Among these, and 'strongly influenced by Information Age rhetoric', as Prusak correctly put it, is

> . . . the confusion extant within the business community between the machinery that manipulates information (computers, software, etc.) and the information itself. Within many firms it is assumed, however false this picture may be, that the information technology (IT) organization, having the word 'information' in its title, therefore is responsible for information provision, quality, and relevance within the organization. This assumption is quite pernicious, since the IT organization usually manages only about 10 percent of the potentially useful information within most organizations and has little or no interest in the unstructured information world. Within many organizations, this lack of interest in the great mass of nonstructured information has led to a strong sense of dissatisfaction with the IT organizations and their usurpation of information within their title. (Prusak, p. 80)

Obviously, if this particular paradigm is going to be shifted, it is up to the information services professionals, the specialized librarians, to bring about the shift, and Prusak recognizes this very opportunity:

Ironically, just as many firms are turning away from a technology-led information polity, many librarians have vigorously jumped upon this very technology bandwagon as a source of ideas about what firms need in the way of information services. (Prusak, p. 80)

Which means, of course, that the information services manager takes advantage of this opportunity to shift the old paradigm, the one that erroneously established that information technology has to do with 'information', to a new one in which the authority for acquiring, organizing, managing and disseminating information is best left to those who understand its value, the uses to which it is put, and the service values that influence how (and indeed, whether) customers will seek information through the established information services providers. We have a situation where the people who understand the mechanics of information transfer are very skilled, and those skills are vital to the successful achievement of the organizational mission, but as far as determining *what* information is required, and how best to provide it, the information services workers are the ones who can bring to senior management the guidance they require for shifting organizational information paradigms.

Undifferentiated service/contingency service

Another of the influences which Prusak has discerned, and one closely related to the work that F. Woody Horton has done in establishing how organizations view information and how paradigms can be shifted, has to do with the service aspect of library and information services work. Commitment to service is praiseworthy, and it is what librarians are famous for, but in today's information marketplace a lack of discrimination in defining just what the information services operation should and should not do is a problem, and a paradigm that itself must be addressed. Prusak describes it this way:

When we look at the collective self-image of librarians we find that they have two central components: undifferentiated service and a strong bias toward a contingency approach to information acquisition and distribution. Unfortunately, these two attitudes are countercultural in most businesses today. To try to maintain universal service in this age of dramatic downsizing and margin pressures seems doomed from the start and is being abandoned by most other corporate functions. Yet many corporate librarians burn the midnight oil struggling to continue serving everyone, even with cut budgets and severely reduced headcounts. There are very, very few useful things one can do with information in serving a client-base of several thousand. Yet this is precisely the position of many corporate librarians. As far as the warehouse mode of information storage (be it warehoused on disks or actual hard copy), this, too, is drastically inappropriate in a just-in-time world. Far better would be to acknowledge, as Peter Drucker proclaims, that every manager should be responsible for his or her individual information management and have the librarian become an internal consultant in helping them achieve this end. (Prusak, p. 80)

What is happening is that a new era of information services is beginning, in which the customer is steadily becoming more and more authoritative and the role of the provider has become more and more service-oriented. The information services paradigm is of course changing to match the times, and the models for information services organizations have also evolved. The requirement now is for information services professionals to look at and understand the role of the paradigm in their work, to choose from the historical models and the current paradigms those components that continue to be valuable and simply shift the paradigms to a new and more relevant point of view. There is no other profession or field of work that has before it such an outstanding opportunity for a new paradigm as librarianship and information services has. Society today is anxiously seeking leadership in this remarkable new age of information. It will be telling, indeed, to find out if librarianship and information services will provide that leadership.

References

Abram, Stephen. 'Sydney Claire, SLA Professional Award Winner 2005: Transformational Librarianship in Action.' *Special Libraries*, 84 (4), Fall, 1993.

Barker, Joel. *Paradigms: The Business of Discovering the Future*. New York: HarperBusiness, 1993.

Hafner, Katie. 'Wiring the ivory tower.' *Newsweek*, January 30, 1995.

Hammer, Michael and Champy, James. *Reengineering the Corporation: A Manifesto for Business Revolution*. New York: HarperCollins, 1993.

Horton, Forest Woody Jr. *Extending the Librarian's Domain: A Survey of Emerging Occupation Opportunities for Librarians and Information Professionals*. Washington DC: Special Libraries Association, 1994.

Matarazzo, James M. and Drake, Miriam A., eds. *Information for Management: A Handbook*. Washington DC: Special Libraries Association, 1994.

Piggott, Sylvia E.A. 'Why corporate librarians must reengineer the library for the new information age.' *Special Libraries*, 86 (1), Winter, 1995.

Prusak, Laurence. 'Corporate librarians: a soft analysis, a warning, some generic advice.' In Matarazzo, James M., and Drake, Miriam A., eds. *Information for Management: A Handbook*. Washington DC: Special Libraries Association, 1994.

'Sylvia Piggott at the Bank of Montréal: reengineering information services for the 2nd era of the information age.' *InfoManage: The International Management Newsletter for the Information Services Executive*. 2 (3), February, 1995.

Thornton, Paul B. 'The seeds of positive growth.' *Personal Selling Power*, November/December, 1994.

Chapter Five

Setting the entrepreneurial standards

When it is time to do something different the entrepreneurial manager should be thinking about entrepreneurial standards. What goals does he want to achieve? Who are the people – the information stakeholders – who will be involved in this activity? How far is he willing to go to achieve the identified goals, and how cooperative will the stakeholders be? These are questions all information services managers must ask as they put forward the standards that are required for success.

Think about a fairly large engineering firm, an organization that has as many as 250 or 300 projects going on at one time, usually at sites throughout the world. There are, in fact, some seventy offices located in different countries, and while the vast majority of these (fifty-seven, to be precise) are located in the United States, Australia and Canada, the others are situated in developing countries where the company is heavily involved in working with government to build the engineering infra-structure they require. None of these offices has a technical library or information resource center, as such, although many of them have collec-tions of materials and reference works for use as needed. Obviously, without any professional information services strategy or management, the level of service in each of these operations varies widely, and to all intents and purposes staff are left to their own devices when informa-tion is needed. As is usually the case in such situations, the users have over the years developed all sorts of ways to acquire the information they need.

At the company's central headquarters there is a legal library with a staff of nine, including a law librarian as the departmental manager, three professionally trained librarians, three paraprofessional assistants and two clerical assistants. The manager reports to the company's chief informa-tion officer, who is also responsible for all automation services for the company: for records management, corporate archives, and public rela-tions and internal communications. Certainly this is a progressive and forward-thinking CIO, for during the five years of her employment, she has instituted major changes in the information structure, and all units throughout the world are now in immediate contact with one another via e-mail, and all records and archives – including project files – are being digitized or scanned and transferred to a CD-ROM format. She is a firm believer in the benefits of an integrated information system, having stated publicly to all information stakeholders within the company (and that includes just about everyone), that she would like to see every employee have access to seamless information delivery at his or her desk within the next five years.

The change to something different, instead of simply improving something that already exists, has come about through the entrepreneurial efforts of the legal library's manager. Typically, the move in this direction was the result of a crisis, an almost disastrous event that would have caused major information problems within the company. The crisis was precipitated in the legal library, which had been perceived throughout the organization as a *de facto* corporate library (that is, existing to offer *all* types of library services to all units of the company); the point had been reached where there was so much work that it simply could not all be done. The library staff were constantly prioritizing and re-prioritizing; essential planning and day-to-day work were neglected; and staff morale was at such a low ebb that the manager was faced with either a walk-out or a mutiny. As she discussed these matters with the CIO, the initial reaction was along the lines of 'Well, it's a library, and you've got to provide the users with what they need'. At the same time, though, it was clear that the service was deteriorating, and the connection between the value of the external information provided and the internal information needs was becoming more and more clear. The company's employees needed both to do their work, and they did not appreciate having to go to many different sources to acquire it.

The law librarian, being something of an entrepreneur by nature, immediately began to think about the situation and recognized that her obligations for responsibility, performance and control, when linked to her natural innovative attitude and her propensity to take calculated risks, positioned her ideally for solving this major problem. Senior management was looking into the option of outsourcing the legal library, and requiring each of the company's other units to be individually responsible for providing their own information solutions. It was a short-sighted and counterproductive idea, and one not supported by the CIO, but until she herself could come up with a better solution it was being seriously considered.

Working with those members of her staff whom she had identified as also being innovative and risk-taking in their approach to their work, and bringing all staff members into the project as commentators, ideas providers and representatives of the customer perspective, the manager was able to devise and eventually put before senior management a plan which, while initially expensive, would solve the company's information problems and permit that seamless transfer of information the company required. The key to the plan's success was striking in its fearlessness, and the risk the library staff took in putting it forward was major, for it involved two significant components that would affect every aspect of their work: first, the legal library would be dissolved as a unit and in its place a corporate information services unit would be created, under the direct management of the CIO. This would include a unit for acquiring and disseminating external information, and the products and services now provided by the legal library would be folded into it, but it would also provide the products and services required by other units that had over the years so clearly made their needs known by going to the legal library. It would be a corporate information center in the true sense of the term. At the same time, however, all services would, wherever possible, be provided electronically, so that external services would be just as available as internal information was on its way to being. All information services would be linked, and no employee would be further away from the information he or she needed than the computer on his or her desk.

At the same time, recognizing that except for the information services employees, no-one in the company was particularly interested in information services as a discipline, the library manager put forward a proposal for 'kiosk' and 'electronic hotline' information advice. In each department or unit large enough to afford it (with the decision being based on size of staff and information requirements, as determined through intensive and specific audits of their information needs, and not upon willingness or ability to pay), provision was made for a specialized information services employee, whose duties and training were chiefly focused on providing information advice, a sort of one-stop customer service checkpoint where any employee who needed information could ask for and receive guidance on how to find it. Sometimes this advice would entail additional training in one of the electronic media; at other times it might involve nothing more than a conversation and a query directing the employee to a source. For those units where such a service was not required, there would be an electronic communications service with a direct e-mail connection to a team of information specialists who could provide advice (and who would also act as back-up for the staff members manning the information kiosks). It was obviously an ambitious plan, but it recognized – and required that senior management buy in to – the value of information in the achievement of the company's goals. Once that recognition and commitment were made, the risks suddenly seemed minimal and well worth taking.

How much risk is 'acceptable' risk?

There's no question but that risk is a part of any entrepreneurial activity, but as has been mentioned earlier, calculated risk is easier to handle. For most librarians engaged in an innovative activity, the risk is usually subsumed into the 'best-case' scenario, in which the services or products to be introduced have been 'market tested'; or at the very least, some level of approval has come to the librarian's attention and there is not a great deal that can go wrong.

Still, there are those occasions when the risk is higher, and as exemplified in the case study just described, the librarian and his or her staff might stand to suffer some harm. Whether the decision is irreversible and the harm serious, as Drucker has described his second type of risk, there is, nevertheless, risk involved and it is up to the library manager to determine whether it is a risk worth taking.

In his writings about the subject, Donald Riggs (1987) has successfully linked strategic planning and entrepreneurship in librarianship, and up to a point his understanding of the connection between the two is applicable in almost any library or information services situation:

> Strategic planning and entrepreneurship share many common characteristics. They both focus on systematic innovation and both are opportunity driven. Calculated risk is an important ingredient in both processes. Risk is managed by utilizing a structured plan that identifies and provides for contingencies. Both processes look critically at present ways of doing things and are not timid about bringing forth innovative ways of doing things better. Furthermore, strategic planning and entrepreneurship should not be perceived as cure-alls for library issues, but they can be described as means for the reassertion of an innovative climate in the library construct. (Riggs, p. 42)

It was in the planning that the manager of the legal library turned what could have been major risks into calculated risks: first she sought and obtained the support of not only her own manager but also her own staff, giving them ownership in the product that would result from their efforts. Certainly the more innovative staff took to the challenge just as she did, but even those who were not so entrepreneurially inclined were given the opportunity to visualize just how good the information services operation could be. Significantly, by bringing in her staff, the manager effectively positioned them to share the risk with her, so that they too would lose something if the endeavor failed. They were willing to take that risk, for they had been convinced that the change would be for the company's – and their – good. Indeed, one of them was heard to say 'Why not? Things can't get much worse' (Figure 5.1).

In fact they could get much worse, and part of the impetus in a situation such as this one is related to the dangers involved when they do.

The manager of the legal library could see that some of her staff were ready to resign, rather than to continue working under the current conditions. As she put forth strategies for improved services, she saw that the risk involved more than simply making a bad situation better: there was an opportunity to do something entirely different, as far as information services in the company were concerned. This library manager fits into a pattern that has often been discerned among innovative management in public sector organizations, with which librarians often identify and

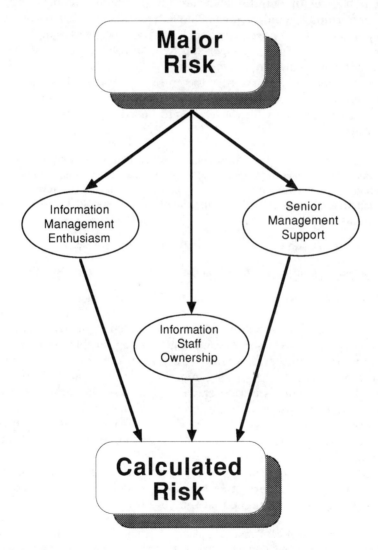

Figure 5.1   Use management support, staff ownership, and your own enthusiasm to change major risk to calculated risk

to whose philosophies of librarianship as an opportunity for 'doing good' they are often drawn. It is easy to see how the motivation that directed the manager of the legal library would not be monetary or economic, but rather, as Sarojini Balachandran (1989) has described it, 'a sense of achievement or a sense of creation' (Balachandran, p. 69). Information services practitioners, and librarians in particular, are driven to achieve, and for this library manager the overwhelming difficulties were merely difficulties to be turned into opportunities. Balachandran also suggests that public sector entrepreneurs are often attracted to new projects by the opportunity acquire power and exercise it. In this particular case, the pursuit of power was tangential, for the risks were simply too great: it truly seems as if the manager and her staff wanted the organization to have better information services.

We mustn't lose sight of the risks, however. While Riggs has suggested a useful connection between strategic planning and entrepreneurial thinking for librarians, in the case study used here there is a parting of the ways:

> Strategies set forth by entrepreneurs will contain more risk than those introduced by non-entrepreneurs. Entrepreneurial risk is not gambling. Proper handling of exposure to loss is part of managing entrepreneurial risk. Librarians engaged in the management of risk should keep in mind three rules:
>
> Do not risk more than one's library can afford to lose;
>
> Do not risk an extraordinary amount of the library's resources; and
>
> Consider the odds before committing resources. (Riggs, p. 44)

Certainly Riggs' recognition of what is called 'calculated risk' – that 'entrepreneurial risk is not gambling' – is applicable to librarians and other information services workers, but in this extreme case the possible payoff was well worth risking more than the library could afford to lose. The situation was desperate, and it was the timing of the risk that made it worth taking. As the library manager developed her plan it became clear that this was one of those situations that fairly defines Drucker's third type of risk, i.e. the risk is great but one cannot afford *not* to take it.

The final result, of course, would have been reliably predicted by Riggs, for he is absolutely correct as regards the success that the combination of planning and entrepreneurial thinking brings to an enterprise:

> Entrepreneurship and strategic planning bring notable changes in the library's mission and general operations. Entrepreneurs tend to create a degree of discomfort for those librarians who resist change. The discomfort can result in positive results for the library, if it is handled properly. A library that is

resistant to change, thereby dampening the entrepreneurial spirit, will be the least likely to cope with continuing and rapid change. For libraries to survive and flourish they must not only accept change, but must also incorporate mechanisms to attach themselves to the concept of change. Libraries in general are not change makers. They are usually characterized as having clearly defined goals and objectives in terms of delivering a service, and are often functioning quite well at meeting these goals/objectives. They respond rather than initiate, drift rather than decide. They need more reasonable adventurers.

Coupling entrepreneurial activities with strategic planning ensures that a control mechanism will be in place during modifications in existing library practices. . . . (Riggs, p. 48)

For many in the library and information services field, however, there is yet another level of risk that must be addressed which is not quite the same as Drucker's third type. This is what might be called 'total risk,' that is, those occasions when the risk of doing something is so great that not only will the decision be irreversible, but failure will result in 'serious harm'. These are the occasions when it is necessary to put one's job on the line, and while most of them involve moral or personal beliefs (reporting an illegal activity, for example), there are plenty of other occasions when such decisions must be made and most of us don't take the risk. Two examples come to mind: in discussing the role of the librarian in a renovation or building project, a group of museum librarians were shocked to be told by a focus group of architects that their input into the planning process was so important that they should be willing to put their jobs at risk to be involved in the project. While most museum directors and curators, to say nothing of their boards of trustees, would consider the librarian's involvement to be something of a nuisance, the architects made it clear that the librarians knew how information was managed and how the library functioned. The directors and trustees would be concerned only with how things looked and the architects were insistent that the librarians put themselves forward in this situation.

A similar situation occurred in an insurance firm, where the librarian discovered that a consulting group was studying information services. From what she could gather from gossip, she feared that the company library would be closed. Instead of doing anything about it she simply worried, and of course her worst fears were realized. If, on the other hand, she had taken some aggressive action when she first heard about the project, discussing the matter with her supervisor and offering to cooperate in the study and even to participate in the expected realignment of information services, she would have been able to survive the change and would not have lost her job. It was a risk worth taking: she would have little to lose and much to gain; as it turned out she only lost, and she had taken no risk at all.

The requirement for information policy

In terms of the role of the information services unit in the company or organization, an acceptable level of risk becomes less of a concern when the organization has developed and adheres to an information policy. For many managers in the information services field, an understanding of and interest in the various aspects of information policy planning, and using these to think about how information policy might determine the success of information services provision and their future management, is necessary. There was a time when information policy was the province of those in a position of some authority to determine how information is regulated. This has changed: now, it is recognized that every organization requires policies for the management and use of information, just as they do for financial planning, human resources, strategic management and the like.

While much attention is given in the professional media to the subject of information policy, most of it seems to be directed at describing specific components of information policy which are desired or required in one or another information arena. In order to think about information policy as a subject in itself, it is necessary to think of information, and particularly the role of information, in a much broader sense. It is here that we use the definition of 'information services', which seeks to be inclusive and which includes the various 'subsections' of information provision and management as it is practiced in our society today.

As for a definition of information policy itself, several authors have addressed the subject, and one of the most helpful is Elizabeth Orna. It should be pointed out that when Orna refers to the 'enterprise' for which the information policy is created, she is deliberately using a term which includes any entity which has a claim on information study or information management. As she puts it:

> Readers will notice that . . . I normally use the word 'enterprise' rather than 'business' or 'organization.' I have done this because what I have to say is relevant to all kinds of places where people work with each other and with information; not exclusively those which make a product or sell a service. And I have a liking for the word because it does suggest people taking initiatives, and that is the essential starting point for an information policy. (Orna, p. 14)

Although Orna's book is about information flow in organizations, it is easy to read into her comments the idea that *all* organizations, including all those that deal with information, can and will benefit from an understanding of *enterprise information policy* as defined by her (Orna, p. 19). For example, the foundation of an enterprise's information policy is 'The enterprise's overall objectives, and its priorities within them', and, according to Orna, enterprise information policy itself defines:

- The objectives of information use in the enterprise
- The priorities among them
- The technology for information management
- The systems for information management, who manages them, and their responsibilities
- The enterprise's resources of information, and its resources for managing them
- Criteria for monitoring information activities.

Orna describes information policy as a dynamic tool which can be used:

- To relate everything that is done with information to the enterprise's overall objectives
- To enable effective decisions on resource allocation
- To promote interaction, communication, and mutual support between all parts of the enterprise, and between the enterprise and its 'customers' or 'public'
- To provide objective criteria for assessing the results of information-based activities
- To give feedback to the process of developing the corporate policies of the enterprise.

Information strategy, then, as defined by Orna, becomes 'the detailed expression of information policy in terms of objectives, targets, and actions to achieve them, for a defined period ahead. Information strategy provides the framework for the management of information'.

Finally, in her analysis of information policy, information management is defined as 'the application of an information policy in order to meet information objectives within the overall constraints of available resources'. In Orna's definition, information management is concerned with:

- How information is acquired, recorded and stored
- How it flows through the enterprise
- How it is used by the enterprise
- How people who handle it apply their skills and cooperate with one another
- How information technology is used
- How the budget is spent
- How effectively all these information-related activities contribute towards the objectives of the enterprise.

There are very real societal reasons why an enterprise or community should wish to become more involved in establishing and adhering to standards of information policy, and useful guidance has been provided by David Bender, Sarah Kadec and Sandy I. Morton in a book they wrote in 1991. They have wisely pointed out that because information 'will be at the center of business and society in the twenty-first century', the environment of those who work with information will be influenced by a number of factors, and each information services manager must be able to recognize and be prepared to work with these factors. They include:

- continued growth in the amount of, and demand for, information
- the intellectual and economic value of information
- increased interdependence among information users and providers
- global orientation of information
- acceptance of, and dependence on, technology
- partnerships between information professionals and users
- partnerships with creators of information
- the development, implementation, and alteration of national and international policies and laws, and
- decreased availability of financial and human resources

(Bender, Kadec, and Morton, p. 2)

It should be noted, however, that in the various descriptions of information policy, the language of the definitions often changes, and information services managers must be alert as to what it is they are trying to establish and how they propose to describe their efforts to the organizational decision makers. For example, as Orna describes information policy, she is quite literally defining what an information policy *is*. Other authors and commentators skip the definition of information policy as such, and find themselves including in their definition *desirable components* of information policy as they wish to see it defined in the particular contexts with which they are concerned. Decision makers in organizations, it should be remembered, while often lacking in the information services professional's knowledge of information *as a subject*, are not at all uncomfortable with theories about information practice and have long ago formed their own opinions. To attempt to bring them into a political understanding of particular principles of information policy, rather than to enlist their interest in and support of the creation of an information policy as an entity in itself, is dangerous and not to be undertaken lightly.

A first distinction must therefore be made in any discussion of information policy, and that is whether the discussion is to center around the structure, desirability and role of information policy *itself*, or around the structure, desirability and role of *specific* information policies related to *specific* information environments. It is my contention that an understanding of the general principles of information policy as described by Orna (but recognizing variations required by each specific information entity) can be used to design, create and ultimately implement an information policy for any organization or enterprise. Such an understanding serves to level the playing field for discussions about specific information policies.

Recognition of the need

Although much attention is now being given to the subject, most 'enterprises', to use Orna's term, do not have information policies. In fact, the idea of preparing for, studying, discussing and formalizing an information policy is probably, for most managers, a time-consuming and ultimately thankless task. Unless one has some compelling reason to look into information and how it is handled, indifference usually wins out over other concerns, usually directly related to the success of the enterprise.

Yet there are valid and responsible reasons for looking at information policy and establishing such a policy where it does not already exist. Certainly Orna's first list in her 'definition' offers plenty of good reasons for the establishment and implementation of information policy (particularly in enterprise-specific terms). In fact, our society and the times we live in, already being dubbed the information age, demand that our leaders think about information policy. At a presentation in 1989, at which the subject under discussion was the economics of information, one of the speakers, Dong Y. Jeong quoted from B.D. Ruben a statement that fairly summarizes the current information situation:

> Information has become an increasing important marker of our age and our culture. Perhaps reflective of this, the term is used to refer to an ever-growing domain of products and services which were previously referred to with distinctive terms. The telephone business has become the information business; electrical and phone hook-ups are now information systems; 'news at the top of the hour' becomes 'information at the top of the hour'; statistics and data are now information. Libraries are described more and more in terms of information providing and administration functions are described in terms of information resource management and information policy. (Ruben, p. 231)

Similarly, the emerging discipline of information resources management (IRM) provides direction as we think about the need for information policy. Described as 'a movement in the government to manage information and make it available to the people of the United States', IRM isn't just about government information but concerns any kind of information services management that involves *really* large blocks of information. With its emphasis on the client, its empowering and decentralizing management structure, its integration of *all* information as its primary task, and its commitment to automation and electronic data transfer to provide better information products and services for those clients, IRM looks at information in management terms that practically cry out for the establishment of policy, regardless of the information entity under discussion. The 'principles' of IRM, as they are called, make it clear that serious information services management calls for serious information policies:

- Information is a resource. Like other resources it has value and can be managed
- Information gains value with use
- Since information gains value with use, it should be available to the broadest possible audience
- Information should be organized to meet the needs of the user; organizations should be organized around the flow of information
- Work will be fundamentally transformed if: information is managed as a resource; information is organized for dissemination; work is organized around information flow

(Megill, p. 5)

There are, it would seem, any number of reasons why an enterprise might want to establish an information policy, and Orna has included several in her definition. However, beyond these are other concepts which might be considered with some benefit. For example, liability/protection issues come to mind when we think about information policy in terms of large organizations, simply because in our litigious society it makes good management sense to have on file a set of guidelines for how the organizations will act or react when questions of information services

ONE. Codifies the Ideal.

TWO. "For the Common Good."

THREE. Liability / Legal Protection

Figure 5.2   Why an organizational/institutional information policy?

management come up. Obviously many organizations base their information policies on what is required by law: tax and accounting documentation, human resources files, etc. On the other hand, when it comes to determining how information will affect (or is *desired* to affect) the success of the organization, the establishment and implementation of information policy is frequently a haphazard affair. As far as the information stakeholders are concerned, however, the sooner an information policy is established and implemented, the more comfortable those stakeholders are in their dealings with information as a resource in their work (Figure 5.2).

When considering the role of information in an organization and the need for an information policy, the discussion moves to a much higher plane. For one thing, many people involved in information services management are quite comfortable with the idea of seeking the ideal in the work they do, and much energy and effort is put into looking at information services management in terms of just how good it can be. They do not always achieve these ideals, and for many of them the realities of information services management, with its frequent dependence on other, frequently external, authorities for resources and support, an information policy provides a proper platform for the codification and documentation of ideal goals. Such thinking is naturally behind much of what is done in the movement toward the establishment of information policies in organizations.

This leads comfortably to another of the basic considerations in the establishment and development of an information policy. 'For the common good' is a label frequently misapplied in society, but the achievement of the common good is a fundamental reason behind the consideration of an information policy, regardless of the information entity. In a company, for example, success and the achievement of a profit can be related to the use of information, and the literal 'value' of information policy can be identified and analyzed. In a community, however the 'common good' is defined, the information structure of that community (including not only its libraries and the educational structure, but community records, archives, historical documentation, planning, legal, and other records) can be directly related to the success of the realization of that 'good'. The existence of a community information policy will obviously guide those responsible for the management and provision of information services toward its achievement. On a larger scale it is the desire to realize the 'common good' that leads people to seek the establishment of national and international information policies.

In the move towards establishing and implementating an information policy there are certain questions that should be addressed, and the entrepreneurial librarian will want to think about these. They can be categorized as follows:

Stakeholders and players. Who should be involved in establishing policy? Is the establishment of information policy the particular purview of information services staff, or should other members of the organization be involved? How are users – the information customers – represented in the process? Do they speak for themselves? What about the 'information indifferent' – the people who don't care about information (even though they use it, in one form or another, all the time)? Are they and their information needs recognized as the organization moves toward the establishment of an information policy?

Barriers and enablers. What forces within the organization, institution or enterprise prevent the establishment of an information policy? Can these barriers be surmounted? What effort is involved? Are there disadvantages to having an established information policy? On the other hand, what forces require or demand the establishment of an information policy? Can the entity operate successfully *without* an information policy?

What kind of policy for whom? What are the differences involved in designing information policies for an organization in the public sector and a company or other entity in the private sector? What local, state, regional, national and international issues must be considered in the establishment of information policies? How are such issues as the concept of

Who are the information **stakeholders**?
The information **players**?

What are the information **barriers**?
Are there information **enablers**?

What kind of information policy for **whom**?

Who are the **subgroups**?
Who are the **individuals**?

Are there **private agendas**?

Figure 5.3   Establishing information policy: the questions to ask

intellectual property, the ownership of information, cultural differences, language, sovereignty rights, etc. handled when the subject of information policy is discussed?

The role of subgroups, private agendas, etc. All organizations and enterprises have within them groups with specific agendas. How are these incorporated into planning for information policy? How are the specific information requirements of these subgroups addressed? What about private agendas – are the people who have these agendas powerful enough in the organization to thwart the efforts of the organization at large? (Figure 5.3).

Certainly, other questions, 'categories' and concepts will come to mind as these are considered, and all of them should be brought into the discussion of information policy. The establishment of an organizational framework for the design, creation and implementation of information policies is of critical importance as information services practitioners look to the future, and certainly the entrepreneurial librarian must incorporate the components of information policy into his or her information services strategy. With open discussion, the full and frank presentation of ideas and concepts, and an honest recognition that the creation and existence of information policies is, indeed, 'for the common good', today's information community can provide that framework for the future, and the organizations and enterprises for which they provide information services will benefit.

Establishing standards is the purview of the entrepreneurial librarian, and all those who learn how to determine the levels of risk acceptability in their organizations, and who combine this with a determination to establish and implement an organizational information policy, will find themselves positioning their information services units in the forefront of organizational growth. It is a position to be earnestly sought, and it is definitely worth the effort required.

References

Balachandran, Sarojini. 'Entrepreneurship in libraries.' *Library Administration and Management*. Spring, 1989.

Bender, David R., Kadec, Sarah T., and Morton, Sandy I. *National Information Policies: Strategies for the Future*. Washington DC: Special Libraries Association, 1991.

Megill, Kenneth A. *Making the Information Revolution: A Handbook on Federal Information Resources Management*. Silver Spring, Maryland: The Association for Information and Image Management, 1995.

Orna, Elizabeth. *Practical Information Policies: How to Manage Information Flow in Organizations*. London and Brookfield, VT: Gower, 1990.

Riggs, Donald E. 'Entrepreneurial Spirit in Strategic Planning.' *Journal of Library Administration*, 8 (1), Spring, 1987.

Ruben, B.D. 'The Coming Information Age: Information, Technology, and the Study of Behavior.' In B.D. Ruben, ed. *Information and Behavior*, Vol. 1. New Brunswick, NJ: Transaction, 1985 [quoted in 'The Nature of the Information Sector in the Information Society: An Economic and Societal Perspective.' *Special Libraries*, 81 (3), Summer, 1990.]

Chapter Six

Convincing the nay-sayers

If an information services manager decides to embark on an entrepreneurial approach it will soon become apparent that there are surprising barriers to his success. Expectations about the information services unit's role in the organization or community will vary among the people with whom he comes into contact in his managerial capacity. While it makes no difference what sort of unit he is responsible for, what does make a difference, and affects his ability to be as entrepreneurial as he would like to be, are the different expectations that people have about what the information services unit should be doing.

At the risk of giving prominence to the negative side of the picture, it is necessary to acknowledge that many people do not like the idea of an entrepreneurial approach to information services management. The reasons are not particularly important, although they should be identified and recognized, but it is essential that the information services manager should be able to identify these people (I call them 'nay-sayers'), identify the barriers that they can be expected to erect, and, most important, be prepared to establish within the organization or community the specific information values that lead these people to judge the success – or lack of success – of the information function. Two factors contribute: the value of information and the levels of service identified and expected by information stakeholders.

Information value within the organization/community

It is now accepted in the information services field that support for the provision of information services (of whatever kind) correlates directly with the value of that information to the organization or community. It is therefore imperative that information services managers have a clear understanding of the value of the services he or she is responsible for providing. To obtain that understanding, the manager must be continually identifying the purposes for which information is required, evaluating the effectiveness of information delivered in aiding those purposes, and monitoring how that information affects organizational or community success. Here are the questions the information services manager should ask when attempting to establish the value of information:

1. Who are the information stakeholders – the information customers – in the organization or community? Much attention is being devoted in the information services field to the information audit, and for a very good reason, for without knowing who uses information and how it is used, the organization or community is operating in a sort of information limbo. The information services manager must send her staff out into the enterprise to identify those people who are using information and to ask them how they use it in their work.

There is an example to illustrate the importance of this activity. Take the records management unit in a fairly large private research organization. The operation is well funded, has been in existence for nearly a century, and grants for research are given annually to a respected body of scholars whose work then becomes the basis for important decision making in the world of finance, investments and global development. Obviously, the records management system is an important part of the organization's structure, for not only are there legal and regulatory requirements concerning the grants, but the records unit also provides the 'corporate' history of the organization. In reality, however, only a small percentage of the organization's fifty or so staff members ever have need to access grants records, and when they do, the information comes to them relatively quickly and in a format that is easily matched to their needs. So there are no complaints about the records management unit; it's there and it does what it's supposed to do.

From the point of view of the unit's manager, however, there is much that could be done to improve services, for she is not satisfied with the speed of delivery and she is certainly not satisfied with the number of staff she must employ in order to have the records organized, stored, retrieved and disseminated. In fact, senior management in the organization often question the resources required for the operation of the records unit, and there are frequently times when funds become scarce and records management staff are laid off or vacant positions not filled. Of course the work suffers, but as there is not a concerned 'public' which places a high value on the information supplied by the unit, there is little reaction and the records manager is perceived as simply 'whining' about lack of staff, just as everyone else does when there is a cutback.

By taking an assertive, entrepreneurial approach to the problem and sending her staff out to interview the people who use the records, or by asking them about the quality of the service when they request information, the records manager is able to supply senior management with *factual* evidence of the value of the information that is her responsibility. To do so, however, requires that the records management staff identify the information stakeholders, that is, not only the *direct* consumers of information from the unit, but others throughout the organization whose decisions and actions are affected. Program officers, for example, perhaps may not themselves come to the records manage-

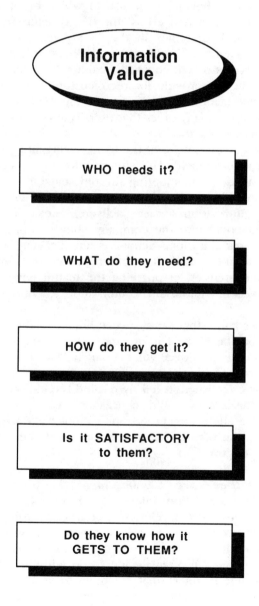

Figure 6.1

ment staff with specific queries, but as information is procured for them, they use it to determine actions that affect the organization's success as a whole. By working with these people the records manager is able to establish the value of the information provided by her unit. In doing so, she has identified the information stakeholders in her organization.

2. What are the information needs of the stakeholders? Information value is linked to the use to which the information will be put and how important that use is, and that is determined by the people who require the information in the first place and how they themselves value that end use. While it is gratifying for librarians and other information services practitioners to establish high standards about what they will or will not provide for their customers, from the customers' perspective such standards are irrelevant. The best way to illustrate this is to think about the many times that users request an information service or product, and when they realize that it is going to require a special effort, turn away with a wave of the hand, saying airily, 'Oh, don't bother. I didn't need it that much'. This situation frequently occurs in a special library, when a user, remembering the old adage about finding anything you need to know in a 'library,' walks in with a request that is inappropriate to the information services delivered there. For example, a staff member might come into the company library to find information that he can give to his child for a school assignment. On being told that the information can be found at another library, he simply shrugs and leaves with no intention of pursuing the matter any further. The information need was not important to him, and the value of the information was nil.

On the other hand, that same special library might have a user whose job depends on the kind of information she is able to procure through the library, and this employee will become an avid advocate of the library. Indeed, the existence of the library is linked to her success in her work, and as she has established in her own mind the kinds of information that are available there, she is able to organize her work around that information. As far as she is concerned, she cannot place a high enough value on the importance of the library, for without it she would not be able to do her job (Figure 6.1).

3. How are these needs being met? The process of information delivery can also affect how information is valued, and the cost to the customer (i.e. convenience, relevance, delivery format, speed of delivery, and any financial costs) is an important part of how information needs are valued. Here again we come up against the 'too much trouble' value judgment, for users will often decide to do without the information, or to change the line of query that led them to seek a particular information service or product, rather than expend the energy or time to follow through on the original query. In a magazine publisher's editorial library, for example, the staff might receive a request for a journal article that an author 'needs' to see. He has asked that it be faxed to him at his office, which is on another floor of the building. When told that a paper copy isn't available but that he can come to the library and consult the CD-ROM product, and then, if he wants to keep the article, print it out himself, he decides not to use the article in his research. It's 'too much trouble' to obtain it, and obviously its value to him is minimal.

For other information stakeholders, particularly senior management who have resource allocation responsibility and who are themselves responsible to the organization for how resources are used, the value of the information to the enterprise is based solely on what it costs to provide it. In one major financial institution, the manager of information services and his organization approach this delicate subject quite directly:

> ... attention to hard data is what makes information services management work in the organization. Willner's not interested in some 'idea' about information services costs; he wants to know specifics, just as his managers do. When he arrived at Lehman Brothers four years ago, there were some 30–40 lines for charging back costs. Now there are over 300, counting some of the service agreements that have been included in the various reorganizations and sales that have taken place in that time. By concentrating on real dollar expenditures (and by quantifying savings when they occur), Willner and his people are able to provide management with financial information that reflects accurately what it costs to provide information services. And that accuracy is paramount, at least in this operation.
>
> It comes, Willner says, in understanding what he refers to as 'the landscape of the place.' Here he's not talking about the usual concepts of corporate or organizational culture, those now almost overworked ideas about 'fitting in' in order to be successful. For Willner, the 'landscape' in a company is more an understanding of where you work, of what the information services operation does.
>
> 'It's understanding what you are going to tell your manager about the operation,' he says, 'of determining what your managers need to know about information services.' And then, of course, conveying it to them. ('Defining . . .,' p. 3)

4.   Are these customers satisfied with the information services and products they obtain from the unit? Value is also related to how well the information services unit provides the information that the stakeholders require, and this is where customer expectations often conflict with what is or is not available. For example, the author described above had expected a paper copy of the journal article he 'needed' to be easily obtained in the library, and when this was shown to be a false expectation, he was able to do without the article. On the other hand, information customers are often sorely disappointed because their expectations do not match the reality of what is available, and it is then that they express dissatisfaction with the information services unit. Such expectations are often built into public perceptions of the concept of a 'library', as has already been mentioned. For example, a public library user who is accustomed to a high level of information delivery in the research institution where he is a senior staff member, discovers that instead of being handed a piece of information – which is what happens when he needs something at the research library – he is directed to the library's OPAC, a shelf of reference books, and a collection of CD-ROM products; this customer is going to register disappointment that his needs are not met. In fact, they could have been, but his expectations of what the library could provide did not match the procedures required for obtaining that information in that particular library.

The reduced value of an information transaction is not always the result of a customer's unrealistic expectations, however. There are plenty of times when the customer has every reason to believe that her information needs will be met, and while some part of those needs is met, she is still left with an information need. Such occasions occur most often when the information staff are very busy, when there is too much work for the information services unit to handle effectively, or when the information services employee simply reduces the information need to match what is easiest to provide in the way of a response. At a very fine medical library, long reputed to provide the very highest levels of information on a variety of medical specialties and offering a wide range of information services to the public as part of its community effort, a call came from an enquirer asking if she could be sent some general information on the subject of osteopathic medicine. She was a real estate agent, and she needed some basic background material before she proceeded to visit and work with a group of osteopathic practitioners in her community, who had invited her to help them plan for their future real estate needs. She asked her question and was told that there was information on file and it could be sent to her. When she asked if it could be faxed to her in time for a meeting the next day, she was informed that this wouldn't be possible, as the information was in the form of a booklet that could only be mailed to her. She gave her address, and as she replaced the receiver she realized that she had been deceived, for the information would not get to her in time to be of any use, and she had, in effect, wasted her time. A more aggressive enquirer would have requested that the pamphlet be photocopied and the photocopy faxed to her, but the information interaction went so smoothly that she simply didn't think to ask for the additional service she needed, a service that the information provider would have considered value-added but that the customer thought of as necessary and basic. If the information employee had suggested the service, of course, the value of the transaction would have been saved; as it was, it was lost.

5. Are these people aware that they are information stake-holders and that their success is connected to the quality of information they acquire from the information services unit? It is not unusual for information stakeholders to be surprised to find them-selves characterized as such. Many people take information for granted, and one of the major difficulties the entrepreneurial information services manager will encounter in attempting to lead the enterprise in the estab-lishment of an information policy is to convince senior management that such a policy is essential. Why? Because the managers themselves don't question the value of the information: it is always 'there'. How it gets 'there' frequently comes as a surprise to them, and when they are asked how they obtain the information they need, they usually reply with some-thing along the lines of, 'Well, I ask Fred' (or Susan or Tom . . .) meaning that they simply rely on someone else. Thus the value of the informa-tion primarily concerns how that other employee values information, and what he or she does when the boss needs information and it isn't avail-able through one or another of the usual channels. Therefore, while senior management are very much information stakeholders, their 'stakeholder-ship' is intimately bound up with that of the people who actually procure the information for them.

For the entrepreneurial information services manager, the problems arise when the information stakeholders do not like the idea of entre-preneurial information services. Regardless of their role in the organization such people can effectively prevent an entrepreneurial approach to infor-mation management, and can do much damage to the organization's information infrastructure. They must be convinced that the entre-preneurial approach is the best approach for the organization or community, and convincing the nay-sayers begins with identifying them and bringing to their attention organizational and community values about information. If the information products and services that are provided are designed to fit within these established and agreed-upon parameters, the information services are contributing to the success of the enterprise. If, then, there are people who oppose success in the delivery of these information services and products, it follows that they are opposed to organizational success.

Levels of service

There is frequently confusion within an organization or community about what kind of information service is to be provided. This is usually based on mixed signals that are sent by organization management, by informa-tion services staff, and by customers in their expectations of the information services unit. What is required of the entrepreneurial manager is a specific codification of the levels of service that will be provided, agreed upon by both senior management and the information services manager; they must also be defined in the mission statement and the strategic plan of the unit itself. Ideally, of course, these levels of service are publicized to all constituent user groups, but if they are not formally publicized they must at least be securely understood by staff so that appropriate responses can be made to potential customers, so that their expectations will be matched to the service that is actually provided.

Levels of service can be described in a number of ways and have been written about elsewhere (St. Clair, pp. 56–60). It should be noted, however, that agreement on the levels of service to be offered is critical in the establishment of the unit's role within the organization or community, and while most entrepreneurial information services managers understand the differences between the 'types' of levels of service, senior management do not, and will require guidance as they and the information services manager come to agree about what services are to be offered. Therefore, it is wise to put together a set of guidelines to which both parties can refer.

Such guidelines will, of course, include the standard levels of service commonly accepted in the information services community, with such distinctions as (for the materials collected or acquired for customers) minimal, basic, support or research-level collections and services. From another point of view, however, decisions will be made about the customers who will use the information products and services: information repackagers, problem solvers, decision makers, those who help others, and 'creative' information customers who look to what are referred to as 'expansive' information products. The information itself must also be considered, and decisions must be made as to whether the operation is to be concerned with factual information, qualitative information, synthesized information, 'how-to' information, or some other type of information; as to the frequency with which it is needed (hourly, daily, weekly, monthly, annually); as to how fast it is needed; and of course how it is to be used. All of these criteria must be deliberated and will influence decisions made about the delivery of information services and products within the organization or community.

There is yet another category of service level that must be considered: it grew out of studies of specialized librarianship several decades ago, but it is still useful for the entrepreneurial librarian and his or her senior management to incorporate into their planning. This is what might be characterized as a 'delivery' level, and for many library and information services operations today these criteria are worth considering. In looking at an information services operation, the manager of the department and his or her managers must agree on whether the information delivery process is to be passive, moderately active or active, and this decision will directly affect the services as well as customer expectations about what services are available.

It would be tempting to dismiss passive and moderately active information services, for in today's high-powered and fast-moving information environment anything less than active would be perceived by both management and customers as retrograde. In fact, especially in specialized librarianship and certainly in traditional librarianship (as exemplified by many public libraries and the libraries of many academic institutions), there is an aversion to an information services operation that is too active, and many of the customers who use these services are seeking a passive or moderately active level of service. The decision that the managers must make is whether the organization or community can afford the luxury of providing the facilities for such services, for while they are perfectly valid as sound levels of service, for the information organization seeking to provide the fastest and most up-to-date service, managing a passive or moderately active unit would seem to be something of a contradiction.

In fact it is not. When we consider the end-user phenomenon that has had such success in the information delivery process in the last decade, what we have is a passive level of service: the user does not come to the information services unit for his information needs, or at least not for those that are available directly through his desktop computer; and when he has a question about those services, if he cannot obtain assistance through the vendor he might approach the library for help, in which case the level of information service moves up to the moderately active standard. Much the same thing happens in a public library, where the user starts in the reference room with the usual encyclopedia and directory-type materials, moves on to journal articles and/or books from the stacks, and then perhaps goes to one of the librarians and asks for further assistance. Here again the customer is seeking no more than a passive level of information service until his needs change, and then, for him, a moderately active level is sufficient. He does not need to have the library's staff address his requirements with an active level of service.

Once levels of service have been agreed upon, and matched to the value of information as it is perceived within the organization, the entrepreneurial manager can then proceed to determining how to deal with the nay-sayers. For now an information commitment has been established, and the manager can move forward in bringing her entrepreneurial management approach into the delivery of information services and products for the enterprise.

Management

If entrepreneurial information services management is to succeed, it must have the enthusiastic support of senior management. The best route to that support is to bring the concepts of organizational information policy to management with the firm recommendation that a policy team be appointed to look at information services needs. There are many reasons why management might be nay-sayers in information matters, and the best list is provided by Elizabeth Orna, who points out that although information professionals understand and work with the concepts of information services management all the time, they are not generally understood by senior management. She lists the obstacles that information services managers must overcome if they are going to persuade senior management to buy in to the development of an information policy:

> Managers usually have a thin and impoverished understanding of what 'information' means in terms of the organization or business.
>
> So they have made no attempt to work out what information the organization needs to survive and prosper.
>
> They have little idea of the relevant information that is available, and still less of its potential values.
>
> They fear being overwhelmed or drowned in information, and so find it reassuring to believe that what they already use is enough, and that justifies unwillingness to invest in new information.
>
> They are not usually good at seeking appropriate information for making decisions – either they look for it too late and haven't time to absorb it, or they adopt the Procrustean tactic of cutting the problem to fit the information available.
>
> They identify information with information technology, and this leads them to the dangerous belief that the 'right' system/software/hardware will do the thinking they have failed to do (including the thinking they should have done about selecting and installing the technology!).
>
> They tend to be obsessed with the 'executive toy' aspect of information technology instead of with the key business issues which it might help to solve.
>
> All this is often compounded, in the current turbulent situation, with something close on panic that blocks even rudimentary thought . . . the paradox that organizations in this situation both need maximum information, and at the same time tend to destructive information politics that inhibit sharing and using information to overcome dangers.
>
> (Orna, pp. 196–197)

Having identified the obstacles, it is not such a great leap to work out which steps are necessary to win management support for an organizational information policy and, with it, an entrepreneurial approach to information services management. The first step, according to Gifford Pinchot, is to identify someone at the senior management level who can serve as a 'sponsor' (as Pinchot calls it) or who, at least, can be a go-between to enable the information services manager to get to senior management with the idea (Pinchot, pp. 143–145). In most organizations this is the CIO, simply because this person understands the concepts, the technology involved and the philosophy behind entrepreneurial information services management. Recognizing that bureaucracies generally reject anything new, the sponsor will work with the information services manager to ensure that the political framework is in place before taking the concept to the final decision makers.

According to Orna, there are four essentials that are required for success in developing organizational policies: top management commitment, a good success record for the information services unit and its employees, identifying the positive and negative forces within the organizational culture, and a carefully chosen team for policy development (Orna, p. 200). These can be illustrated with an example: not long ago a large professional association located in New York City determined that its various information-providing units were almost literally falling over themselves in their attempts to deliver information products and services – of many different kinds – to a membership base that exceeded 200,000 people worldwide. There was no organizational information policy, but the association's library manager had been charged to look at the information services picture, with the expectation that 'something would be done' about this chaotic and expensive situation. Being something of an entrepreneur herself, the librarian did her study, hired external consultants to conduct a thorough information audit of both membership and staff information needs and expectations, and determined that what was needed was an organizational information policy with a senior management officer, a Chief Information Officer, with overall information responsibility for the association.

Her first step was to find a sponsor, although in this case it couldn't be another information professional, since there was no one with that expertise at the senior management level. As it turned out, however, the Vice-President for Finance had authority over many information functions at the association, including MIS operations, and he was interested in the assignment the librarian had been given. After a series of meetings with him, and having determined that she had his support to move forward with her work, the librarian sought top management support for the idea of an association-wide information policy that would enable the association to move toward the eventual realization of a seamless, integrated information services operation. Recognizing that she had a rapport with the V-P, Finance, she began a series of carefully planned, carefully choreographed meetings with him, bringing him in to the picture and demonstrating to him not only how some of her ideas would benefit the organization as a whole, but specifically how he himself might benefit. In other words, she saw an opportunity to benefit from his interest in the ideas that she was putting forward, and she took advantage of that opportunity.

Once he began to see the advantages of the programs she was talking about he, of course, began to speak about them himself, and in a very

short time had built up a contingent of advocates for improved information services, and in every conversation on the topic the librarian's
name was brought in. She was obviously by now the point person for
this activity. It was not a mantle she wore with any disdain, for as an
entrepreneurial manager herself, her department was well managed, was
perceived as such throughout the association (particularly by the staff at
the association's central headquarters, all of whom relied on the library
for nearly all the information they needed for their work), and its success
record was good.

The next step was to identify the positive and negative features of the
organizational culture, and this the librarian and the vice-president were
able to do, for they realized that the organization had a reputation for
being very modern and forward-looking in much of its work. In its field
of specialty, its members were thought of as 'leading the way'. Its training
programs were the most technologically advanced, its financial operations
were exemplary and its track record for membership support for new
approaches to organizational issues was famous for being so advanced.
There were, nevertheless, negative features: the chief executive had been
with the organization a long time, and found that rousing himself to
enthusiasm for new ideas was a lot of bother; as a result there was a
disproportionate turnover rate in senior staff positions. At the same time,
many of the middle-level staff were not advancing, since the chief executive did not, as a rule, promote from within, so most middle-management
people had been in their positions far too long and weren't interested
in changing the status quo. Nevertheless, the librarian and the vice-president saw these features as challenges to their ability to move a new
information structure into the organization, and they set about to change
the organizational culture so that it would be receptive to the new
program that they had in mind.

It was not an easy task and there were nay-sayers at all levels, but the
technique they used is right 'out of the book', and is the fourth of Orna's
tactics. The librarian and the vice-president simply talked with people
they knew to be influential in the information arena within the association, and as these people came to appreciate what was being put before
them, they found themselves being part of a well-chosen team that would,
eventually, have formal responsibility for developing and implementing
the new information arrangement.

There were three groups of people who would need to be convinced,
and with much planning and cooperation the librarian and the vice-
president together were able to envision for each of them just what
improved and enhanced information services would do for the association. For management, it was necessary to put the improvements in terms
of a more effective and more efficient (i.e. cheaper) service, and this they
were able to do by demonstrating how a reorganized information infrastructure would create better information delivery for all concerned.

At the staff level there were two groups of people who had to be convinced, and it was important that the information services staff be convinced of the advantages of a new style of management. The information staff included not only those who worked in the association's library, but employees of other information services as well whose managers who reported directly to the Vice-President of Finances. As far as information services personnel were concerned the primary objections had to do with changes in their jobs; once they were assured that the proposed changes concerned work patterns and information delivery, and realigned positions, not reduced ones, it became easier to persuade these employees to support them.

Other staff had different perspectives, concerning services and how a new information infrastructure might affect the delivery of the information products and services the staff has become accustomed to. When informed that no services would be reduced but that current services would be enhanced and more services offered, the customers were able to accept the idea of change (Figure 6.2).

Who To Target	**What They Want**
Organizational Management	Effectiveness Measures Cost Reductions
Information Services Staff	Job Enhancements Job Realignments (Postive Ones, Not Negative)
Information Customers	Better Services (*Not* Reduced Services)

Figure 6.2   Winning advocates

Did it work? Of course it did, because the librarian and the vice-president, working together, were able to use their knowledge of excellence in information services management in tandem with the organization's need for improved information delivery. They presented that combination of resources to all information stakeholders in the association, and once everyone had been convinced, it was simply the 'right' thing to do to make the change. In fact, to have opposed the change would have characterized the opponent as being opposed to organizational success, and that, of course, is a foolish notion for any employee.

Denying the nay-sayers

Finally, it must be recognized that no matter how well planned and well thought-out the introduction of new or different services can be, there will always be people who are opposed, for a variety of reasons. They may be people who simply cannot deal with change, or they may like the processes and procedures already in place, however cumbersome they may be, simply because they fit this or that 'piece' of their personal agenda. Whatever the reasons, what the proposers of any entrepreneurial managerial program must be alert to is the fact that, no matter how 'right' the cause, that 'rightness' is not necessarily self-evident. The voice of the nay-sayers is almost invariably more powerful than their numbers, and once the few opinion leaders and outspoken critics have been won over, the others with whom they come in contact will follow them. Nevertheless, those who are seeking to bring about change in an information environment must be determined, they must 'hammer away' at the 'rightness' of the effort, and they must be willing to put up with the difficulties and sometimes painful resistance that they come up against. Especially in group situations (staff meetings and the like) there will be people who will clearly attempt to derail the effort, and there will be difficulties in persuading the group to accept the recommended changes, but if the advantages are continuously and strenuously acknowledged, it can be done.

References

'Defining the corporate library: Richard A. Willner at Lehman Brothers.' *InfoManage: The International Management Newsletter for the Information Services Executive*, 1 (8), July, 1994.

Orna, Elizabeth. 'Why you need an information policy – and how to sell it.' *Aslib Information*, 21 (5), May, 1993.

Pinchot, Gifford III. *Intrapreneuring: Why You Don't Have to Leave the Corporation to Become an Entrepreneur*. New York: Harper & Row, 1985.

St. Clair, Guy. *Power and Influence: Enhancing Information Services Within the Organization*. London: Bowker-Saur, 1994.

Chapter Seven
The entrepreneurial manager: authority, accountability, responsibility

Typically, managerial success is based on performance: managers are judged by what they and their staff achieve toward the attainment of organizational goals. Managers of information services units provide information consultations and implement the delivery of information products. For most of us, however, day-to-day operational demands often interfere with our ability to act (i.e. perform) managerially. We must recognize that managerial performance is not necessarily elusive. Successful service delivery and management can coexist. Three elements contribute:

Authority is the power a manager has to give orders, to make decisions about the information delivery process, and to expect obedience in the performance and productivity of one's staff.

Accountability is the manager's own obligation to perform, to carry out his or her responsibilities, and at the same time ensure that the work of the information unit contributes to organizational goals. Related to this is the manager's obligation to instill in information staff an understanding of acceptable performance standards. Every staff member should be willing to sign his or her name to the work he or she does.

Responsibility is the bridge between authority and accountability. Responsibility requires not only that the individual manager has the authority to issue orders, but that he or she is willing to answer to his or her own managers for evaluation purposes (Figure 7.1).

It is generally agreed that a manager's responsibilities fall into four primary categories. In most environments the role of management is to conceptualize and plan the work to be done, to organize that work, to direct the work processes, and to evaluate the performance of those responsible for providing the products and consultations which are offered to customers. The successful fulfilment of these functions requires an understanding and acceptance of the validity of one's authority, account-ability and responsibility. When planning, organizing, directing and evaluating are linked with these management attributes, the information unit is well on its way to achieving success (Figure 7.2).

For success to be assured, however, the information services manager must bring an entrepreneurial perspective to the managerial process. He or she must look at each of the managerial functions and ask very basic questions about that function and what it achieves. Thinking entrepreneurially, the manager pursues what Drucker calls 'organized abandonment' and doesn't shy away from those defining character-istics that Drucker identifies: the entrepreneurial information services manager 'upsets', 'disorganizes' and seeks 'creative destruction'. In other words, the entrepreneurial manager is consciously and actively seeking to innovate; entrepreneurial thinking brings innovation to the managerial process.

This concept is not as radical as it appears to be, for it simply means that the questions being asked are based exclusively on what the infor-mation services operation is attempting to achieve, and in this day and age, with so much flux in delivery patterns for information services, drastic upheaval in the information delivery process is almost expected.

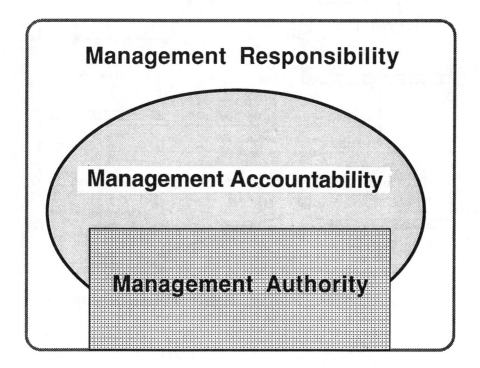

Figure 7.1   Entrepreneurial librarianship: the management perspective

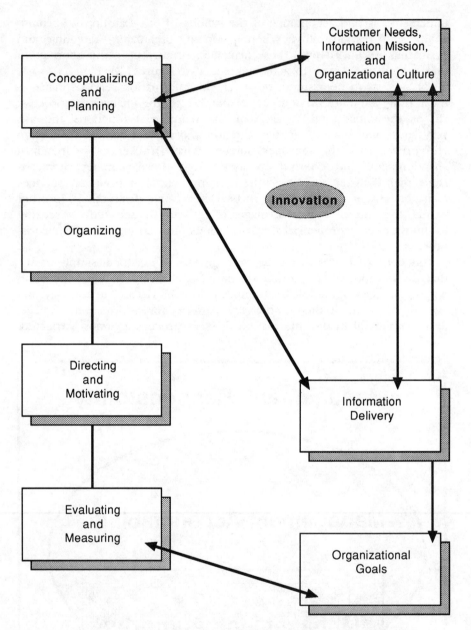

Figure 7.2   The management role in the entrepreneurial library

Certainly in terms of the management of these services, there is (or should be) wide latitude for new thinking and innovative approaches. So in looking at each managerial function the first question to be asked is: Is there a *different* way to do this? And immediately, of course, a second question comes to mind: Why, then, are we doing it this way?

Developing the product/matching the mission

The answer to these questions is found in a review of the role of the operation under discussion. Not 'What are we doing?' but 'What are we *supposed* to be doing?' becomes the guiding question. In answering that question honestly and objectively, the innovative direction of entrepreneurial librarianship seems appropriate and right. In order to develop the information products and consultations that the users require, the entrepreneurial information services manager goes to the users to determine what their needs are.

One of the first things the manager discovers is that a new definition of information services is required. As discussed earlier, in today's information environment a broader, more inclusive picture is called for, and the standard information products and services of the past must be augmented with new ones unthought-of as recently as a decade ago. Additionally, information customers are now seeking *consultations*, and this is assumed to be one of the standard components of the information service today. Information customers want to be able to come into a library or other unit and discuss their specific interests with information professionals. Frequently, these customers are not seeking a specific information product or service: what they most often need is a willing ear, an expert who will take the time to listen as they present their ideas and then offer experienced, professional advice as to what the next step might be. This is a new role for information providers (or at least one which is finally being accepted by those with authority over information operations as valid and proper), and one which in most organizations has not been fully explored by either management or the information staff.

It is necessary to establish what is meant by information products and consultations. Using the term to describe the output of an information services operation is risky, since 'information services' has become the catchword to identify a broad-based concept of information work that includes all forms of information delivery, and because the term is also used in many organizations to identify functions related to the management of information technology. Yet each of these activities is a 'service', for those people employed in these functions are providing a 'service' to their identified constituency.

In most information units a great variety of information services can be identified, although most usually fall into one or another of a very few categories: user services and technical services, the former being those that Ellis Mount (1995) has identified as information retrieval, the alerting of users to current data of interest, the circulation of materials, and those services relating to the writing and preparation of data for use (Mount, p. 108). A subtle refinement of this definition calls attention to the most visible of user services, the answering of reference queries and the compilation of citations (as well as document delivery, when required) through a literature search. In some information services units, of course, there is a slight difference in the format of the information being sought (as in a records management unit, for example, or in the delivery of archives in an archive department).

What is popularly known as 'technical services' are those background activities that relate to the organization of information. These services must obviously be attended to, and Mount wisely points out that users of most specialized libraries have no notion of what these activities are, but if they were not performed satisfactorily those same people would be very aware of the situation (Mount, p. 132). Such technical services include cataloging and indexing, the ordering and processing of materials, and their preservation and care. While administrative tasks *per se* do not necessarily require interaction with information customers, as with technical services, the absence of these activities, or their completion in a less than satisfactory manner, would affect the level of customer interaction and negatively affect the delivery of services.

The entrepreneurial information services manager begins by conceptualizing, organizing and planning a program of information delivery based on the needs of the organization of which the unit is a part. To arrive at an information policy for the organization (and to determine the role of the information services unit in the implementation of that policy) a variety of formal and informal procedures will be utilized, including personal observation, conversations and meetings with the information stakeholders, the information audit/needs assessment, and similar techniques. The entrepreneurial manager then works within that policy to create new information services or enhance existing ones.

There are, of course, organizations where there is no formally structured information policy, but even there, there is a *de facto* policy, whether it is acknowledged or not, and it influences the delivery of information products and consultations in the organization. In these situations, the entrepreneurial library manager simply determines what the information policy is and organizes her information strategy so that it fits into it. So whether it is formal or not, the organizational information policy is the first place for the entrepreneurial information services manager to look in determining what steps to take to establish or enhance an information operation.

In most cases, of course, there already exists some form of information delivery, and the initial task for the entrepreneurial manager is to look at the existing information structure and determine what works and what doesn't. She will then proceed to bring about whatever changes are required, and it is here that she will take on the Druckerian mantle of 'organized abandonment' and 'creative destruction'. An example illustrates the process. In this, a large research institute devoted to regional planning, the person with managerial responsibility for the information services unit determines that a total restructuring is called for. He chooses to invoke the precepts of entrepreneurial librarianship to achieve his goal, which is the creation of a specialized library that will provide his customers with the exact information products and services they need for their work. This librarian has already determined that the library as an agency for the delivery of information is failing. It was created several decades earlier, when studies in regional planning were just beginning to be developed as a separate discipline in the field of public administration, and its basic design was as a traditional storehouse-type library. Its mission was to collect all that could be collected in the subject and to have those materials (in those days, in hard copy only) organized and retrievable for those who would need them for their work. The library was designed purely as a reactive support operation, and was so regarded by the institute's management, with the attendant minimal support and even more minimal interest.

For many years the library generally provided the materials its users needed, and its collections were regarded as among the finest in its subject field. From the mid-1980s on, however, the library began to be perceived as problematical, and while no one could state exactly what the problems were, there began to be a feeling of unease about it. In 1990, the library director retired and a new director was hired. Interestingly, one of the first observations made by the new librarian was that the library's decline seemed to be coinciding with the hiring of new institute staff, many of whom were recent attendees at fine graduate schools, where they had had excellent research facilities available to them. As they had been trained in more modern and more advanced research methods, using the latest equipment and retrieval methods, they found that they had little interest in seeking information through the resources of the institute's old-fashioned library. After having been employed at the institute for the better part of a year – during which time he had made careful observations of user expectations and the levels of service they were receiving – the new director presented a case to senior management and his staff for the implementation of a full-scale information audit. The audit – which took the better part of four months to complete – confirmed his observations, and it became clear that a major change was required.

At this point, the library director had several options before him. He could attempt to repair some of the problems; he could call in an external consulting team to help devise new delivery mechanisms that would preserve the best of the old library service and attempt to combine it with information delivery systems that matched the expectations of the institute's younger, newer staff; or he could take an entrepreneurial approach and seek a complete restructuring. He chose the latter, for he felt that, despite the extra effort involved (especially in persuading some of the senior staff that a library is not a storehouse of books and reports), he would be not only organizing the library to provide what the customers wanted, he would be positioning it as a essential element of the organization's structure, a unit that would be recognized for its critical role.

The library director began by looking at what he himself was authorized to do. He knew that the process would be disruptive, and he felt that he needed to be authorized to do the things that had to be done. So he looked at his role in the organization and at the levels of authority, accountability and responsibility that were expected for a manager in his position, and determined that he could move forward. His authority related to his power to give orders, to make decisions, and to expect obedience from his staff. A look at his own job description, at his ranking in the organizational hierarchy, and at the people at his own managerial level with whom he came in contact assured him that he had the authority to make drastic changes in the way information services were delivered in his department.

As far as his accountability was concerned, he recognized and understood his own role in the management structure, and he knew that large-scale decisions affecting information delivery were taken by his own staff only in consultation with other managers whose employees would be affected by any changes. Nevertheless, with a clear understanding of how the work of the information unit contributed to organizational goals, it was not difficult to obtain support and even, in some cases, enthusiasm for the changes he proposed.

Finally, the manager recognized that it was his responsibility to the organization and to his customers that provided him with the proper framework for making his drastic changes. He recognized and accepted that he had authority to issue orders, and he was more than willing to accept the accountability required for such efforts and to answer to his own managers for the success of his and the department's efforts.

As an entrepreneur this librarian was taking a totally innovative approach to the reorganization process. He became totally customer focused. While the library had always declared itself as being user-oriented, such a designation was more often than not a misrepresentation, for more customers were disappointed than ever had their information requests filled. The new director, however, with the results of his information audit always readily available, would bring up 'the customer's perspective' or 'the customer's point of view' at every opportunity, to the extent that within a very short period of time everyone in the institute knew that his primary objective was the development of an information delivery system that would meet customer demands. No longer would customers be told that such-and-such a document could be obtained 'next week', or to drive to a nearby university, 'where as a member of the institute's staff you have library privileges', or that this or that request would be denied because 'it's not in the budget'. Instead, even before he had restructured the library, the new director had created an ambience that declared to everyone that the delivery of information was taken very seriously in this library, and that the customer's information requirements would be honored.

The innovation didn't stop here, however, for the director determined early on that people in the institute were interested in information matters, and he decided to exploit that interest by inviting users, managers, and even identified non-users, to participate in focus groups where he invited them to begin with the proverbial 'blank sheet of paper' (Hammer and Champy, 1993, p. 49). They were to discuss, openly and frankly, any ideas and concepts about the delivery of information that came to mind. And the more preposterous the idea, the more likely it was to have value. The results were phenomenal. What the new director and his staff (and the institute's management) learned was that the library currently in place was not responsive to their needs, and that most institute employees saw no need for or had any interest in its being a warehouse of books and materials. By the same token, however, not being information specialists themselves, they had no interest in learning the more esoteric refinements of information retrieval, and were not interested in being end-user searchers with the various databases and other information products that contained the information they needed. What they wanted – and were willing to support, through a departmental chargeback system (which, incidentally, they themselves brought forward in the discussions) – was an information operation that could provide them with the information they needed, or, at worst, *very specific* directions for obtaining that information elsewhere. What they did not want was to have to spend time seeking information: they wanted someone else to find it for them or lead them to it, and they were willing to pay for that service.

Obviously, the institute's information stakeholders were calling for a wholesale restructuring of the information function, and it was up to the library director to determine how to effect this major and unsettling change. With this charge in hand, the library director was able to work to conceptualize and organize a plan for library and information services that met the stated requirements of the information users. This was not necessarily easy, of course, for there were risks involved. Some senior management feared that such innovative library management would end up costing more than the current system, so the library director and his staff had to be particularly careful in working out financial projections that demonstrated that the new service would be more cost-effective than the old. Also, some of the library's users – some of the long-term staff at the institute – liked the library as was and were uncomfortable with the idea of reorganizing what was (for them) an information resource that – despite its high costs and proven ineffectiveness for the general institute population – provided them with what they thought they needed. These people, too, had to be reassured that their needs would still be given serious consideration, or that the very least they would be directed to another library that would provide the kind of services they had become accustomed to.

That this entrepreneurial effort was destined for success was determined by a number of factors, not the least of which was the library director's commitment to the authority of the customer. While he and his staff recognized that they themselves were the information experts, they also recognized that their customers were the arbiters of their success. By going to the customers and asking them what they wanted, the library director and his staff were able to organize an information delivery unit that functioned as it was meant to function, delivering the information products and consultations that the users themselves had determined they needed.

It is important to recognize that in cases such as this, the mission of the organization has not exactly changed, but the means for its successful achievement have changed. As younger researchers and other information stakeholders came to work at the institute, their methods were not the same as those of their predecessors. Thus the library director is not attempting to match the mission of the library to the mission of the institute, but rather to that of its users. Of course, their goals and the goals of the institute were the same; it was the library's goals that needed to change.

Managerial authority/responsibility

In Gifford Pinchot's classic definition of the intrapreneur, such a person is characterized as 'any of the "dreamers who do". Those who take hands-on responsibility for creating innovation of any kind within an organization. The intrapreneur may be the creator or inventor but is always the dreamer who figures out how to turn an idea into a profitable reality'. The entrepreneur is 'someone who fills the role of an intrapreneur outside the organization' (Pinchot, p. ix). For the point he was trying to make, it was entirely appropriate that Pinchot reversed the idea of the entrepreneur, and strictly speaking, in this consideration of entrepreneurial librarianship and innovative management it is 'intrapreneurism' that we are dealing with, for each library manager belongs, by definition, to an institution or organization in which he is 'dreaming'. The point to be made, however, is that the entrepreneurial manager has the *responsibility* for creating innovation, and that responsibility connects with his or her responsibility as a supervisor in the enterprise.

The task then becomes one of connecting managerial authority to one's responsibility for achieving departmental success, which means, in effect, that the entrepreneurial manager has to bring to the workplace leadership qualities that inspire and motivate staff to produce the highest levels of information delivery and, at the same time, to market to users so that they will take advantage of what is offered to them. If the entrepreneurial role is to lead the unit successfully through change, then the entrepreneurial manager's task is clearly identified: he is to be what Scott Shane (1994) has characterized as a 'champion' for his department: 'Research on the innovation process has shown that the presence of an innovation champion – someone who takes a personal risk to overcome organizational obstacles to innovation – is an important part of new business development, new technology development, and organizational change processes' (Shane, p. 397). It is in his or her role as 'information champion' that the entrepreneurial librarian makes the most important contribution, for by establishing an ambience in which staff and users are comfortable with an entrepreneurial approach to information delivery, innovation becomes part of the accepted routine in the information unit.

An information 'champion' can assume many forms, but in the entrepreneurial library or other information delivery operation, specific steps can be taken:

1.   *Develop – and share – an information vision.* Regardless of the format of delivery, it is the manager who sets the stage for the service. As the manager you know what the information unit should be doing and you are in a position to share your vision and enthusiasm. If you think that a 24-hour turnaround time is too long for delivering documents, let your staff know that you think so. Even if there are bureaucratic or other barriers that are beyond your department's control, by sharing your 'ideal' with your staff you might together be able to figure out how to break down some of these barriers. Or they might lead you to others in different departments who can help you implement a faster delivery time.

2.   *Encourage the information staff to contribute to your vision – and reward them for doing so.* It has long been established that self-interest is the best motivation, and Gerald Kushel (1994) has even gone so far as to analyze self-interested motivation in terms of intensity ('how strongly the person wants the reward'), durability ('how long-lasting the motivation is'), motivation ('the time, the place, and the way in which the reward is delivered'), and the perceptions of the person being motivated (the person's 'unique set of values and needs') (Kushel, pp. 65–67).

In an entrepreneurial context the information manager wants the staff to contribute to his or her vision simply because the productivity of the department must be of a high enough level to meet the needs of the

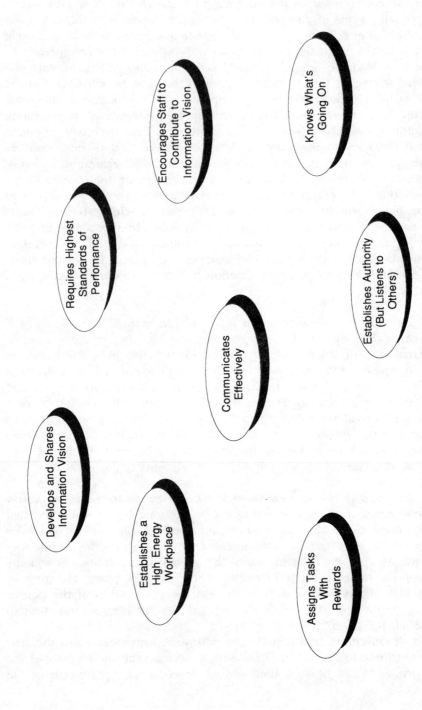

Figure 7.3   The entrepreneurial champion/manager in the information services environment

users. The process of contributing to the vision enables the department staff to be involved (the reward) and positions them to 'buy in' to the success of the department. It is not necessarily difficult, and it requires primarily a willingness on the part of the manager to 'let go', to allow others in the department to take risks. Lois Lesavoy, an independent distributor in New York for a major manufacturing company, and herself a successful entrepreneur, likens the entrepreneurial encouragement a manager offers his or her staff to that of a parent who is willing to permit a child to take risks. 'Taking a risk isn't a bad thing', Lesavoy said in response to a query about entrepreneurial traits. 'When a child has been overprotected and not allowed to test himself, that child grows up with some adjustment problems, having difficulty adjusting to some of the problems that might come his way'. So it is with an employee. If an entrepreneurial manager recognizes that he or she has a staff member who is interested in taking risks, in pushing forward some things that may or may not work out, that employee should be encouraged. Furthermore, the manager has a responsibility to encourage employees to take risks, to give them the opportunity to, as Lesavoy puts it, 'move forward, to operate without a net'. It's an important requirement in today's information services marketplace, and employees want to be encouraged to take chances. Their managers just have to be willing to let them.

3.   Assign tasks that provide rewards. There are few sadder sights than a library or other information services unit in which the lines between 'professional', 'paraprofessional' and 'clerical' employees are so clearly drawn that the rewards all fall to the 'important' staff members and the others are left out. The thank-you from the satisfied user, the interesting but not-too-time-consuming simple reference search, the brief conversation with a user about which other resource unit might offer the best information that is not available here, are all simple rewards that make information employees feel good about their work, but if they're never given the opportunity to perform tasks that offer some intrinsic reward, they aren't going to be very interested in buying into an entrepreneurial role for the unit (Figure 7.1).

4.   Establish a high-energy environment. There's an old idea that a library should be a quiet and peaceful place, the better for users to 'think' about the intellectual activities they're involved in while they are there. This scenario can be taken too far. In today's information picture, people are contacting an information unit for information: the place isn't a 'study hall' (unless it has been specifically designated as such): as a busy information processing and distribution center, the department should have a quality of 'busyness' and high energy. It's not a place to relax.

5.   *Communicate effectively.* The information staff are not mind readers. The entrepreneurial manager takes great care to see that his or her ideas about the delivery of information are clearly understood by all staff, and that each staff member is invited to respond to those ideas. One does not give up one's authority by expressing oneself well.

6.   *Take time to know what's going on – and what you need to be doing.* Although it is important to provide time for your staff to reflect and come up with innovative ideas, it is also important that you as the manager have some quiet time for planning, thinking and otherwise devoting your energies to thinking about that 'best case' scenario for your department. And if you can't find time to close the door during the workday, remember that you're a professional and your hours are not conditioned by the same constraints as those of your staff. If you need to stay late at the office one night a week so you can 'think about things', do so.

7.   *Establish your authority but listen to others.* You are the manager of the department, and you are obviously in charge, but your openness in listening to the opinions of others will go a long way towards helping you establish an innovative environment. If your staff understands your vision of what your operation can do, and if they are comfortable sharing their ideas about that vision with you, they are not going to take advantage of your authority.

8.   *Establish the highest standards of performance – for yourself and for your staff.* We're all human and mistakes will be made, but when they are made, instead of absorbing them into the fabric of the information operation, find out why they happened and make sure they don't happen again. Intolerance of error is not necessarily a bad thing; if your customers aren't getting the information services they need, find out why. You and your staff together can set up processes so that mistakes don't happen.

References

Mount, Ellis. *Special Libraries and Information Centers*. Washington DC: Special Libraries Association, 1995.

Hammer, Michael and Champy, James. *Reengineering the Corporation: a Manifesto for Business Revolution*. New York: HarperBusiness, 1993.

Kushel, Gerald. *Reaching the Peak Performance Zone: How to Motivate Yourself and Others to Excel*. New York: American Management Association, 1994.

Pinchot, Gifford III. *Intrapreneuring: Why You Don't Have to Leave the Corporation to Become an Entrepreneur*. New York: Harper & Row, 1985.

Shane, Scott A. 'Are champions different from non-champions?' *Journal of Business Venturing*, 9 (5), September, 1994.

Chapter Eight

The entrepreneurial workplace

It's all well and good to give attention to the values of innovative thinking in the management process, but there must be a connection between what is being attempted and the projected results. That connection is the information services workplace. It is the day-to-day management of the information services operation, with its specific attention to appropriate workflow processes, staff and management interactions, and above all the authority of the information customer, that determines the success of the information services unit in the achievement of its goals. By understanding what is being attempted in the information delivery process, by contriving and working within a mutually supportive departmental culture, by establishing a recognition of the value of accountability on the part of all staff, and by sharing in the rewards of departmental success when they are achieved, the entrepreneurial information services manager makes an important contribution to the success of the organization of which the department is a part.

Directing the effort/staff responsibility

Obviously a manager directs. Yet the specifics of that role – particularly in the information services field – are often slighted as the manager looks at the goals he or she expects to achieve. All too often, managers 'jump in' without being fully prepared to direct the effort. It is that direction, however, that establishes the entrepreneurial, innovative workplace, and information services managers can look at their directing 'style' for opportunities to bring staff responsibility into the picture. Two qualities contribute, and both are exemplified in the way in which Ann Wolpert manages her operation.

Wolpert is Executive Director of Library and Information Services for the Graduate School of Business Administration at Harvard University, in Cambridge, Massachusetts. When her colleagues speak about her management style, they almost always comment that they appreciate the fact that she is a good listener, that she hears what they are saying and thinks about what her response will be before she gives it. It is not surprising, then, that one very noticeable quality in staff attitudes has to do with staff loyalty, not only to the organization, to the library and information services operation, but to Wolpert as a supervisor. There are approximately 100 staff members at the library, seven of whom report directly to Wolpert herself. Even so, she makes it her business to get to know each of her staff as well as she can. For example, it is her practice, after a new professional employee has been on staff for a while, to take that person to lunch, for part of her job, she believes, is to offer encouragement and to demonstrate to staff that she is aware of the role everyone plays in supporting the vision of information services they are attempting to realize. It helps to give the employee a 'feel' about their place in the organization.

The other quality Wolpert exemplifies is what might be referred to as self-empowerment. This is a concept that first came into play in the late 1980s, when John Nathan made a contribution to *Inc* magazine about the kind of people who succeed as innovative leaders in their organizations (Nathan, 1989, p. 39). What Nathan said was that people who are successful in the management community are 'insulated against self-doubt'. They have a highly articulated vision of the world they inhabit and of how they want it to be; at the same time, they have the energy and the self-confidence to bring that vision to realization. Nathan called this combination of vision and energy a great 'empowerer' and that, if anything, characterizes Ann Wolpert and the work she is doing at the Harvard Business School. With respect to information services, she has empowered herself and her staff to do what Harvard must do to meet the information demands of its constituencies.

Once management has created an ambience that encourages innovative thinking, staff can be expected to contribute to the entrepreneurial picture as well. In fact, the entrepreneurial workplace does not have to be strictly an information delivery operation, for the entrepreneurial employee, regardless of the framework, will work to create an innovative workplace. That is what Doris Small Helfer did at the Teradata Library at AT&T Global Information Systems in El Segundo, California. Although the library/information service is a one-person operation, Helfer is part of a corporate-wide move toward a customer-focused business model, and saw it as her responsibility to view her own customers as the focal point in the information delivery process. By having consultations with information customers about how they used the materials she procures for them, Helfer was able to direct her own efforts at cutting through layers and eliminating duplication and overlapping work. Supported in this area by her own supervisor, who not only encourages Helfer in her innovative progress but also, in effect, stimulates her to push herself forward in this direction, Helfer is able to offer a unique brand of information service that matches exactly what her users need. The payoff is tremendous, for the customer satisfaction surveys (as well as Helfer's performance appraisals) indicate clearly that the people who use her library like what they are getting.

Departmental culture

No matter how open to innovative thinking the support staff is, or how willing they are to incorporate entrepreneurial perspective into the information delivery process, the manager must lead the way (Hagner, 1994, p. 42). Staff must be made aware of and recognize that there is a organizational/departmental 'culture'. and when it is a culture that encourages change, staff must support the need for change. Customers, too, can be involved, but the customer connection must relate to what the department's charge is.

If there are problems, share them. Surprises are not just bad news for managers, they're bad news for employees as well, and every manager's direct subordinates should be given as much authority and autonomy as they can possibly be given. It is important to encourage responsibility in these people, and to encourage them to seek responsibility in the people who report to them. In an intriguing essay on the state of innovative thinking in libraries, Brian Champion quotes William E. Souder and describes the five 'essentials' that are required in the workplace for the cultivation of ideas: sabbaticals, release time, the provision of guidance and guidelines to intrapreneurs, organization idea campaigns and contests, and job rotation, including exposing staff to many diverse work situations. Champion also adds his own recommendation, that 'if intrapreneuring is to function well in libraries it requires at least one other essential: tolerance'. And in seeking to create that idea of an entrepreneurial information environment, Champion adds one further suggestion: 'The five-to-fifteen role ought to be applied to librarians: 5 to 15% of professional staff time should be slotted for the pursuit of ideas in a wide spectrum of interests (2–5 hours a week in a 37.5 hour week)' (Champion, pp. 40–41).

It sounds almost too good to be true. Can it work? There are possibilities. Think about two information delivery operations, both in the same organization, a research and policy development group located in Washington DC. Admittedly, the two information units are different, for one – the organization's records management unit – is concerned with internal information, historical and current data that has to do with the organization's staff, its publications program, its growth and development, its grants funding and similar information. The other unit, the think tank's library, specializes in obtaining external information for various program directors, fellows and others who are affiliated with the organization and frequently need information and research to support the work they are doing.

While the managers of the two departments report to the same person (the Vice-President for Finance), they are managed in completely different styles. The Vice-President herself believes in entrepreneurial management, and has carefully structured the fundamentals of the two managers' jobs so that they are free to run their departments as they choose, with little or no interference from her. She is supportive of what they do, but with a considerable number of other operations under her responsibility she prefers to have the two units (and the organization's MIS department, which also reports to her) as independent as possible.

This arrangement is fine with the manager of the records management unit, who himself is something of an entrepreneur and works with his thirteen staff members to operate a unit that is entrepreneurial in concept as well as in the delivery of information to its users. The staff structure is arranged so that each staff member has full authority to offer suggestions, seek improved methods of information delivery, and to work with users to help them determine what information they need. Through clever and adroit lobbying on the manager's part, he has been able to build up a working arrangement that incorporates the Souder/Champion model. By engaging in an exchange relationship set up with the Records Management Society in London, for example, each of the records management staff is entitled to a four-month sabbatical after seven years of employment. The employee goes to London, works with a similar institution there, and learns about records management ideas and techniques as practised in the United Kingdom. While there the employee works only half-time, enabling him or her to use other time for courses, reading and study, and similar pursuits that 'broaden' the experience so that he or she is better prepared to do the work when it comes time to return home.

Release time, too, is a standard part of the working package at the organization, and all records management staff are encouraged to participate in local, regional, national or international professional activities and, depending on length of service and ranking in the department, time is made available for serving on committees, for the preparation of professional papers and presentations, and similar activities. Ideas campaigns and contests are part of the organizational culture at the think tank, and again time is made available for staff of the records management unit to work with members of other departments in developing organization-wide policies, for committee and group representation, and similar activities, all of which give staff the opportunity to interact with others in the organization and get to know them personally, so that they are better equipped to work with them when they come to the records unit for information.

In an effort specifically directed at creating new programs, ideas and innovations, the chief of the department and his immediate assistant make a point of meeting regularly with various staff members to ask them how the department could better meet its information delivery requirements and what they would do to improve things. These and similar topics are constantly under discussion, and the manager of the department and his assistant have become known throughout the organization for their openness and their receptiveness to new ideas.

Job rotation is a key feature of this department, for the chief feels strongly that all staff should understand how the records program works. The continual review of the retention policy, for example, would normally fall to one or two of the more experienced staff, but it is the department head's opinion that the younger members of the staff – who work closely with clients when they come for information – understand more clearly what the customers' needs are. It does work out that all staff in the unit – including the department head – devote between 5 and 15% of their professional time to thinking about new and different ways to service the clients and their needs. And of course, in such an environment, the 'other essential' that Champion calls for is obviously in place: tolerance of each other's activities is simply part of the department culture, and because a level of respect and mutual consideration is built into the running of the department, each staff member treats the others exactly as he or she would expect to be treated. Every member of the staff recognizes that this is the way people who respect one another work together, for the mutual benefit of the entire group and the department. Institutional support – in the form of departmental support and, when required, support from the senior management – is in place, and the department runs very well indeed (Figure 8.1).

The library, however, does not present such a pleasant picture. The library manager is a martinet in the classic sense of the term. A strict disciplinarian, he believes strongly that the use of his authority is the way to get things done, and he permits no questioning of his authority. As a result, few members of the organization's staff come to the library to do their research, and most of them have long ago figured out ways to use other information-providing organizations to obtain what they need. There is no entrepreneurial thinking in this library: the manager has long ago decided what the users need and the materials he and his staff would be willing to supply, and he brooks no interference.

Needless to say, staff turnover in the library is high, but this does not seem to bother the manager and his assistant librarian, who between the two of them pretty much control decision making for the library. Only the director and the assistant are permitted release time for professional activities, the director on the national level and the assistant on the local level. Other staff wishing to attend or participate in professional

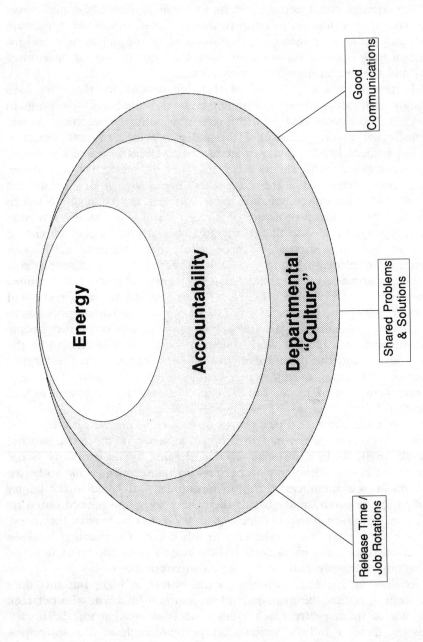

Figure 8.1   The entrepreneurial workplace

activities must take vacation time for the purpose so obviously no-one participates. The idea of sabbaticals doesn't even come up, although the manager was heard to complain at a management meeting about the 'wasted' resources being used to send organizational staff on travel junkets. It was an obvious gibe at the records management chief and his staff and it was wisely ignored. These and similar problems have seriously damaged the library's credibility, and it is fast losing its position of authority in the organization.

So the environment in the library is not a particularly healthy one for either the staff or the users. Obviously, this situation has come to the attention of the Vice-President of Finance, and it will be only a matter of time before serious changes will be mandated, and the library – hopefully – will then be reconstructed according to a more open, customer-focused entrepreneurial style. In the meantime, however, library services remains disconcertingly bad, and users are staying away.

This tale tells an obvious story about how information is expected to be handled in today's information marketplace. It is not difficult to see what the problems are, and it is not difficult to envisage what the solutions should be. Certainly, incorporating the 'essentials' that Champion advocates into an information operation's management scheme certainly makes sense in today's fast-paced, demanding environment, but for many information managers, obtaining support from *their* management might prove to be problematic. Nevertheless, the effort should be made because, as can be seen, in the long run the entrepreneurial, innovative workplace pays off in better service for the customers. After all, they are why the information unit exists in the first place.

Accountability in information delivery

There's a story, probably apocryphal, about the writer who went to the Enquiries Desk at a large public library to ask about a biographical reference book she had used on another occasion. It was getting on for 9:30 pm, the library closed at 10, and the man at the desk was busy with some paperwork. She stood there for a few minutes, and when he didn't look up or acknowledge her, she cleared her throat.

'Yes?' he asked, still not looking up.
'I wonder if you could tell me where I'll find *Current Biography*?' she asked. 'I used it recently to look somebody up, and I need it again.'
Without looking up, the man said. 'We don't have *Current Biography*.'
'But,' the patron said, 'I just used it the other . . .'
Before she could finish the sentence, the man looked up, obviously irritated, and spoke in very curt tones.
'I *told* you we don't have the book.'

End of conversation. End of information transaction. End of that writer's relationship with the library, and probably with any other library unless she is forced to go to one because she cannot find what she needs anywhere else. It's a common problem and, when combined with the number of queries that are answered incorrectly, or the number for which incomplete information is provided, it becomes apparent that there is an accountability problem in much information delivery.

To be fair, such careless information delivery is more prevalent in institutions and organizations where the information does not directly connect to the information provider's work. Certainly in a specialized library or corporate records management unit, where profits or other success depend on the accuracy of the information delivered, accountability is built in. But even then there are plenty of times when an enquirer, often because he or she doesn't know how to ask the right question, and the information supplier doesn't have the time or the skill to determine precisely what is needed, is given a partial answer, and in those situations there is seldom the attention to accountability that there should be. How can this be corrected? Are there specific techniques for ensuring accountability in the information services field?

It is the manager who leads the way in establishing an attention to accountability within the department, and among the various opportunities open to this manager, several stand out:

1.   An 'ambience' of accountability. This is not to say that the departmental manager should be a martinet, but the lack of discipline that leads to a lack of accountability can often be forestalled by establishing, from the very beginning, a departmental 'culture' that requires staff to perform to the highest standards of customer service. This means that much time and energy are devoted to training, and as staff are taught the various parts of the department through which information is delivered, they are also shown that compromises in terms of information delivery are not permitted.

2.   Emphasis on accountability in staff meetings. At the risk of causing embarrassment, when certain procedures are discussed at staff meetings those whose work is not up to the expected standard are invited to discuss how the task could have been performed better, or what the expected outcomes might have been if the staff member had done more than he or she did.

3.   Procedures for handling complaints. While we are aware that most dissatisfied information customers do not bother to let us know when we fail to meet their expectations, as service providers we do have an obligation to listen carefully to those who do complain, to accept that their complaints are reasonable and serious, to discuss the complaints with staff, and to ensure that corrective action is taken. In all cases there should be a complaints procedure, and all staff should be aware of it and invited to participate in an ongoing effort to understand and implement the complaints policy.

4.   Constant reiteration of quality service standards. Every information delivery operation should have a framework for quality service, and at all staff meetings and training sessions this focus must be emphasized. Every employee in the department should be made to understand that 'second-best' or 'acceptable' standards of information delivery are not good enough, and a quiet pride in the level of excellence of service standards should be part of the departmental culture (Figure 8.2).

5.   Built-in follow-up procedures. Entrepreneurial information services managers do not regard customer follow-up as an 'extra', to be implemented as time and circumstances allow. In training information delivery personnel, whether they be database searchers, reference librarians or working with end-users to see that they access information as effectively and as efficiently as they can, emphasis must be given to the end of the activity, after the customer has received the information. As with other tasks in the department, follow-up procedures are required, and employees should participate in the drawing up of these procedures, so that they understand the importance of determining that the customer is satisfied.

6.   Collaborative relationships. While much attention is being given to the advantages of the collaborative workplace, most of it concerns collaboration within the work organization. Equally important, however, is the relationship that grows between customers and staff, and since the major benefits of collaborative workplaces include decision making that is customer-driven, and a focusing of workplace energy on the customer rather than on internal conflicts and procedures (Marshall, p. 7), it is only natural for both users and information providers to tell one another how they are doing in their respective positions. Such collaborative relationships contribute much to accountability, and staff are much more likely to perform well for customers who can be expected to tell them how well they did in providing the information that they needed.

Rewarding the success

Obviously pay is one of an organization's strongest rewards, and when employee benefits and or perquisites are added, the financial inducements can be substantial. Bonuses for specific achievements, and participation in annual bonus programs, are useful. Promotions, too, are an important incentive, and managers must look for every opportunity to promote from within.

In addition to these standard incentives, however, Rosabeth Moss Kanter, among others, has identified that in today's more demanding workplace, more is expected of staff and managers and leaders must find 'new and more effective incentives to encourage high performance and build commitment' (Kanter, pp. 91–92). As Kanter's list has already been explored in another book in this series (St. Clair, 1993, pp. 110–111) it is not necessary to go into detail here, but every manager should recognize that these incentives in 'the new workplace' are just as important for rewarding employees who pursue an entrepreneurial direction as they

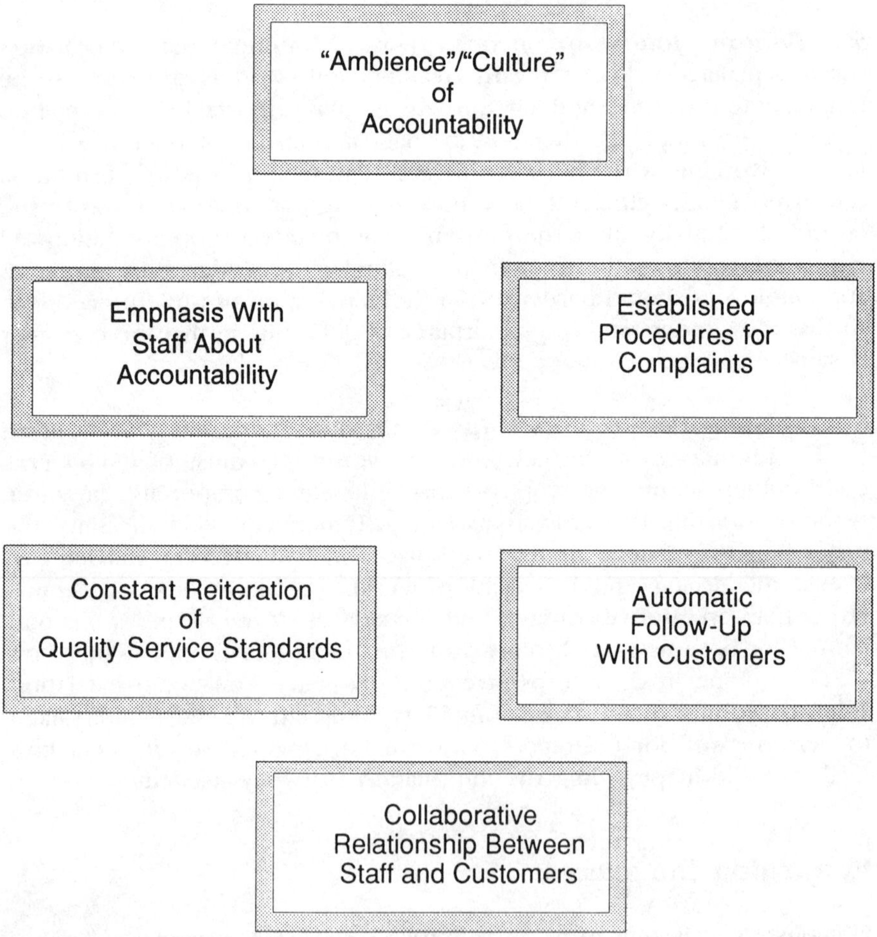

**"Ambience"/"Culture"
of
Accountability**

**Emphasis With
Staff About
Accountability**

**Established
Procedures for
Complaints**

**Constant Reiteration
of
Quality Service Standards**

**Automatic
Follow-Up
With Customers**

**Collaborative
Relationship Between
Staff and Customers**

Figure 8.2   Accountability in the information services environment

are for any other incentive purpose. Kanter's list includes managerial efforts connected to the mission of the department or the organization, since believing in the 'importance of their work' is essential. Kanter also recognizes the importance of what she calls 'agenda control,' wherein the employee is invited to participate in the creation and achievement of entrepreneurial goals, and any effort on the part of management to give the employees 'a piece of the action' is especially beneficial to the organization in terms of staff loyalty. At a fairly large corporate library in New York, the staff were particularly aggressive in helping achieve several new and unusual directions in the company's progress, to the extent that several large accounts were added to the company's client list as a direct result of the library staff's efforts. When bonuses were handed out at the end of the year, the library director was taken aside and told that she was going to be given an additional $10,000 bonus because of her efforts. Recognizing that it had not been a solitary accomplishment of her own, but the result of much exertion on the part of every member of the library staff, she asked the managing director to permit her to submit a list of how the extra bonus was to be divided up, and she worked out a formula so that each member of staff received part of it. Some staff members of course received more than others, for the formula was based on the extent to which – in her judgment – each member had contributed to the task, but everyone received something, and each felt, therefore, that he or she had had a share in the value creation, to use Kanter's term, for the work of the library. Needless to say the staff reacted positively to this action on the part of management and appreciated the recognition.

Recognition does not necessarily have to be in financial terms, but it is an important incentive in the operation of an entrepreneurially managed information services function, and two other of Kanter's new incentive 'tools' build on the concept of acknowledging an employee's contribution. One of the things that employees want nowadays is to learn, and with corporations and other enterprises looking to move to a role as a 'learning' organization, employees are excited at the opportunity to learn new skills and then apply them so that not only does the enterprise benefit, but the employee has positioned himself or herself as a catalyst for the realization of those benefits. In a records management unit where an employee is given release time to learn the theoretical underpinnings of corporate librarianship through continuing education, the company is going to benefit. When the employee is then given the opportunity to work with management to develop an information policy that recognizes the interrelationships between internal and external information, and is permitted to work toward the development of information systems that incorporates that recognition, the employee has contributed to organizational success, an achievement that is not only good for the company but also good for the employee.

Similarly, reputation is an important part of one's professional work, and the opportunity to share with others in the professional community, to build one's reputation as an innovator and entrepreneur beyond the immediate workplace, is an important motivator and one that entrepreneurial managers invoke whenever they have the opportunity. A fine line must, of course, be drawn between those tasks that contribute to the employing organization's wellbeing and those that enhance the employee's professionalism, but it must be recognized by both management and staff that within those parameters it is important for staff to share their experiences and their knowledge with others in their profession. Managers must also understand that reputation is also important within the organization, and every opportunity must be given to recognize individual staff members, through incentive awards, recognition in meetings, and similar activities, for the contributions they make toward the entrepreneurial success of the department.

References

Champion, Brian 'Intrapreneuring and the Spirit of Innovation in Libraries'. *Journal of Library Administration*, 9 (2), 1988.

Hagner, Thomas H. 'How to cultivate company culture.' *Personal Selling Power*, November/December, 1994.

Kanter, Rosabeth Moss. 'The New Managerial Work.' *The Harvard Business Review*, November/December, 1989.

Marshall, Edward M. *Transforming the Way we Work: the Power of the Collaborative Workplace*. New York: American Management Association, 1995.

Nathan, John. *Inc.* 11 (4), April, 1989.

Souder, William E. 'Stimulating and managing ideas.' *Research Management*, 30 (3), May/June, 1987.

St. Clair, Guy. *Customer Service in the Information Environment*. London and New Brunswick, NJ: Bowker-Saur, 1993.

Chapter Nine
Constant improvement, or 'getting better all the time'

Although this is not a book about quality management, one of the basic components of the quality approach to organizational management is a critical element in the pursuit of entrepreneurial thinking. In a famous essay on total quality management published in 1992, Michael Barrier offered a list of four 'essentials' required for a successful total quality program in business. Although all four contribute in one way or another to an entrepreneurial environment, Barrier's attention to continuous improvement is especially relevant. In writing about the continuous improvement of products and services, he asserts that 'TQM is not a static concept; by eliminating chronic problems, it opens the way to never-ending innovation' (Barrier, p. 22–23). It is innovation we are looking for in an entrepreneurial information environment, and it is in the continuous improvement of processes and procedures that entrepreneurial librarianship finds its success.

Most entrepreneurial and intrapreneurial activity is thought to take place in the larger corporate and institutional workplace, and of course that is where most of the work described in the business literature is done, a fact that has been noted by several commentators, including Camille Carrier:

> In recent years, the literature in the field of intrapreneurship has, generally speaking, dealt with the importance of the phenomenon from the point of view of the situation in firms that wish to increase their innovative capacity and thus their competitiveness. Although the concept of intrapreneurship has so far been studied almost exclusively in a big business context, it is nevertheless equally vital for . . . [small and medium-sized businesses], which must also face up to today's increasingly competitive world. However, given the specific nature of smaller firms, it may be that intrapreneurship is developed and practiced differently. (Carrier, p. 54)

Smaller libraries and other information services operations can benefit from the application of entrepreneurial, innovative management. If there is any one point that comes through after a conversation with Gretchen Reed at MVBMS in New York, it's that she has positioned herself, a one-person librarian, and the services she provides as a vital, even critical, component of the company's success. Messner Vetere Berger McNamee Schmetterer/EURO RSCG is one of the most successful advertising agencies in the United States, and as part of the EURO RSCG communications network – the largest agency group in Europe – MVBMS creates advertising for a host of impressive clients. So naturally it's a business in which innovation and entrepreneurial management is encouraged, but even so, Reed – Vice-President and Director of Information Services – has gone out of her way to restructure information services with the information customers in mind. Although most specialized library/information center operations, even in an industry as creative as advertising and public relations, are traditionally expected to be part of Research and Development or a similar department, at MVBMS the information services component of the business has been structured to mix research into a broader, more management-oriented picture. The information services scope has been broadened and, as such, has required that Reed herself move away from the more traditional information-providing service to information policy work. The delivery of information has been structured for the customer, and electronic networking is a critical component, with the company having its own gateway to the Internet and all of the staff, some 300 people, using it. Reed herself operates as a sort of information 'counselor', providing the staff with directions and guidance when they need it and, of course, using all of her professional contacts and personal/professional networks to lead her customers to the information they need. It is not a static environment and it is most definitely one in which the information services operation is expected to perform entrepreneurially.

How using entrepreneurial attributes leads to constant improvement

For the manager of an information services operation who wants to establish an entrepreneurial ambience, there is a list of common attributes which can provide a framework for innovation. These are among those identified, with reference to past research studies, in work that Theresa Lau and K.F. Chan did in using what they term 'the incident method' to study entrepreneurial behavior (Lau and Chan, p. 53). These attributes, while not necessarily original in the entrepreneurial context, are valuable when grouped together. Looked at individually in an information services context, they can provide useful insight and guidelines for the 'entrepreneurially prone' library/information services manager:

1. Innovation vs stabilization. Here, of course, is the key concept that defines entrepreneurial management. As many scholars and others have pointed out, libraries and information services functions are not necessarily the most conducive organizational entities for innovative thinking. Nevertheless, as they broaden into the 'umbrella' construct that has been described earlier, and are absorbed into integrated information schemes, the demand for change – and the concomitant demand for innovation to keep up with changing demands and changing structures – becomes a driving force.

A striking example of such an approach to information services is taking place at Columbia University Health Sciences in New York. There, Pat Molholt, Assistant Vice-President and Associate Dean for Scholarly Resources, is creating an information infrastructure for which the word 'innovative' seems to have been coined. It has a name – CHIPS, the Columbia Health Information PerspectiveS Project – and its purpose is to use technology to link curriculum planning with information services planning. With technology, Molholt points out, the library becomes a true service operation, for it becomes possible to combine the perspective of the teaching faculty with the librarians' perspective. Libraries have always played a secondary role in the area of curriculum support, and by providing workable alternatives for delivering information to supplement the lecture environment (even into the post-graduate phase of the practitioners' careers), the librarians work with faculty to help the institution in the delivery of education, which is, after all, its mission. It is a fascinating prospect for the future of all education, and it is only a matter of time before other fields of study pick up on the idea. Could it have worked before? Probably not, even if it had been thought about, because the technology wasn't there. Now that the technology exists, there is no reason why such innovative linkage cannot take place between formerly disparate activities such as teaching and librarianship. It's an innovation whose time has come, and Columbia University Health Sciences and Pat Molholt are providing a good example of how information delivery in an integrated environment can produce solid, measurable results for the workplace.

2. Informal structure vs formal structure. Certainly structure is required in almost every enterprise, and despite the much talked-about moves to 'flattened' management structures, there is still a built-in hierarchy (if, for no other reason, to enable organizations to meet certain regulatory or legal requirements). Yet innovation and entrepreneurial endeavors die if the structure is too confining and too restrictive. Therefore, even in those situations where structure is required, the wise manager will figure out a way the staff can benefit from a certain level of informality, in order to stimulate creative and innovative thinking.

Consider a hospital library, in which might be found a particular case in point. Required by the hospital administration to offer information services according to a certain schedule (usually along the lines of 8:00 am to about 4:00 or 4:30 pm Monday through Friday), with typical staff limitations it is difficult if not often impossible to 'relax' the management structure so that a more creative ambience is achieved. Certain tasks must be performed each day, each reference employee is required to be present at the enquiry desk for a certain number of hours each day, and so forth. It becomes awkward to change these inhibiting restrictions, yet a dynamic and innovative library manager will want to do so.

As a first step she recognizes what cannot be changed: hours of operation, hours of enquiry services etc. As for the other work to be done, she creates teams that work together to innovate, and outside the required scheduling operations these teams have the freedom to meet and work as they choose. The technical services operations, the SDI and routing services, and all similar processes that are not directly user-'affective,' so to speak, are organized within the various teams, each of which has a team leader or coach whose primary task is simply to see that the work is done. How it is done, how it is scheduled and who does it is not of great concern, either to the coaches or to the manager. As a result all sorts of eccentric and sometimes even unorthodox arrangements come into play (particularly in terms of what are often referred to as 'library routines'), but the other side of the coin is that very creative and innovative methodologies are devised, and quite often these new routines result in better services for the identified user base.

3.   *Reliance on informal methods (or self) vs formal system.*
Similarly, there is a tendency – or so it is supposed – within library and information work to do a job simply because it has always been done, or to do it in a particular way because it has always been done that way. Information services workers (especially librarians, archivists and records managers) seem to have a propensity to avoid changing any methodology that already exists, yet many people working in these fields find themselves frustrated when they are expected to perform their tasks according to certain routines and patterns. In the previous example, the beauty of the working teams is that each team leader or coach is authorized to permit the group to accomplish its goals however it chooses to do so, provided that the end result is as efficient and effective as possible (and it is the user who has the authority to make that judgment).

A process that seemed right for change with one of the working teams at the hospital library concerned the processing and routing of a certain group of monthly technical reports for which the library had a standing order. The reports – published by a committee responsible for the establishment of standards for a category of medical instrumentation – were required by the hospital's Chief Staff Officer but were used by no-one else at the hospital. When the reports came in, they were shelved with a group of materials to be processed and, in turn, keyed into the automated library catalog so that they would appear in the online catalog that was accessible to all employees throughout the hospital. Invariably, because the reports were handed off several times between receipt in the library to delivery to the Chief Staff Officer, there were delays, and someone from the hospital's administrative offices would call each month to see if the report had arrived.

There was a procedure for these technical reports, one that had been devised for all technical reports routed to various staff members in the hospital. The primary difference, however, was that the other reports were routed to a group of individuals and were eventually returned to the library for processing, storage and retrieval (when requested). The instrumentation reports never came back to the library, they were not accessed into the library's report collection, and, most important, no-one cared whether they were available or not, once they had been received by the Chief Staff Officer. How he disposed of them no-one knew; all the library staff knew was that there was a record that the report had been received at the library and that it had been sent on to the interested party. As a team of acquisitions employees went about their work, attempting to devise more efficient methods, it became apparent that the formal method for dealing with this type of acquisition was more trouble than it was worth. One of the team came up with the idea of simply sending the reports on to the CSO. Another suggested that the organization that issued the reports be sent an address change, so that the reports were mailed directly to the CSO. A third suggested that, since the CSO's administrative assistant might not want to keep track of the reports, a call to that person might be in order. The team's coach was asked to make the call, but she felt that doing so might open a discussion that she didn't want to have to deal with, so she simply sent an internal e-mail message to the CSO, briefly outlining the difficulties and noting the recommended change. The message concluded, 'unless you object, we will implement it immediately. Please let me hear from you by 5:00 pm tomorrow if you do not agree with this decision.' There was no objection, and the change took place without incident.

4.   *Preferring changes vs. the status quo.* There are, of course, those who simply prefer change for its own sake, but by and large such employees do not seriously affect the innovation results, and the information unit is probably better off with this type of employee than with the sort who cannot deal with change at all. Nevertheless, the 'change-for-change-sake' employee must be guided, and his or her work patterns must be closely watched so that the ultimate product – the delivery of the information product, service or consultation – is not hampered or interfered in with any way.

In the quest for continuous improvement, the wise manager encourages each employee to think about each process in his or her work and question its validity and its contribution to the larger departmental workflow.

5.   *Loose vs. tight budgetary control.* The financing of any entrepreneurial venture is always a touchy subject, particularly when the staff are not totally convinced of the value of an entrepreneurial approach. Such is often the case in larger public or academic libraries, where the middle management have 'risen through the ranks' and, not being trained as managers, often see their role as more directly related to line management and to enhancing their relationships with line workers than of seeking out and working with institutional or organizational goals. These middle managers often think of themselves as responsible for the line workers, their former colleagues, and 'protecting' the line workers from organizational and/or senior management 'abuses' often becomes their primary focus. In such an atmosphere innovation and entrepreneurial management are difficult to achieve, frequently because financial arrangements must be so controlled that there is no opportunity for 'loose' budgetary control.

Still, there are situations where the entrepreneurial manager has discretion over some parts of the budget, and it is these managers who are able to establish a workplace where innovative thinking can flourish. In describing the intrapreneurial framework, both Pinchot, writing about the business community in general, and Champion, writing about librarianship, emphasize the value of giving the intrapreneur some freedom as far as finances are concerned. Pinchot says that the most tangible form of business freedom is the power to spend money on new ideas without having to ask for permission, and Champion calls an access to funds 'catalytic' in the effect it has on the innovator, and he suggests that financial freedom is the second most important factor in developing the intrapreneurial thinker (he refers to the freedom to do or 'play' as the primary factor) (Pinchot and Champion) . Naturally, as both Pinchot and Champion would agree, money must be kept track of and intrapreneurs must not be permitted to exceed their spending authority, but this requires nothing more than ensuring that such people understand that they must operate within their budgets and approval levels. It isn't a difficult concept to get across, and it can provide a useful built-in check and balance system for the entrepreneurial thinkers.

6.   *Exploiting opportunities vs reacting to problems.* 'Getting better all the time' begins with an understanding of what opportunities are available to the information services unit, and Beth Duston has identified one of the most prevalent of these as the user no-one knows about (Duston, p. 7). During an interview at a major corporation, a staff member described to Duston by the librarian as a 'non-user' of the library indicated that she was, indeed, a user of information services. Both of these people were correct in their assessments. Although the librarian had never seen the employee in the library, the employee was satisfied with the library and the information products and services she was receiving. The library staff created online databases which were accessible throughout the company, and this employee accessed these at her workstation. She also tapped in to the networked CD-ROM operation and, as is typical in many organizations where the research library is open and available to customers after normal working hours, she used library materials after hours. She was, as Duston described her, 'a fugitive library user.' Although she was never seen in the library or counted in any of the library use statistics, the library and its products and services were important to her and valuable in her work.

This is an opportunity to be exploited. The entrepreneurial library manager takes a look at this situation and determines immediately that this employee is accessing only those materials and resources that she knows that she needs. She has no idea what else is available through the library or its resource networks, or the staff's professional networks and connections. As a first step, someone on the library staff determines to interview this employee and inform her about what additional library services she can take advantage of. For example, an interview might determine that what she needs most frequently is an information consultation, a conversation in which she can discuss with one of the information professionals any information problem or need she has. In any case, she (and all others like her in the company who can be identified) will benefit from knowing about the information services, products and consultations available to her, and the library will once again be offering its services to a market that values them.

7. ***Reliance on network vs depending on given resources.*** In today's information community the term 'network' has come to acquire a variety of different meanings, but when entrepreneurial librarians are talking about their networks they are generally referring to two things: the people they know to whom they can go for advice and assistance (and to whom they are willing to offer advice and assistance when called upon), or the vast wonders available through electronic networking. Both are essential in today's information arena, and exploiting these two 'lines' is a critical element in the delivery of information. No-one pretends to be an all-inclusive information provider: every information specialist knows where to look for additional direction. Only those concerned with proprietary information, security and similarly restricted subject areas operate alone, and even many of these are willing to share with others their information resources and guidance, so long as there is no conflict with those that cannot be shared.

Two examples come to mind. Gretchen Reed, described at the beginning of this chapter, has a quick answer when asked how she gets support for the work she needs to do. She relates it to the level of services she provides, pointing out that she cannot be insular in the work she does. She says that she has to be a generalist in her work, and she has to know where to go to find the information the customer is seeking. This is one of the hallmarks of being a professional, and when this is how you've structured your job and your services, the work is going to be supported.

Yet a one-person librarian needs resources, and Reed uses those of an excellent trade association, in her case the American Association of Advertising Agencies, which provides her with access to vast amounts of material without having to maintain collection of her own. At the same time, she makes full use of the Corporate Library Services at the New York Public Library Research Libraries, an arrangement which she characterizes as very satisfactory and one which, is financially very reasonable. Finally, Reed likes to refer to what she calls her 'information partners': friends, colleagues, members of her various professional associations, all of which make up a professional network that she can call on when she needs it. 'You learn to network within the profession,' she says, 'and you learn who is willing to share leads to information, just as you will share with them.'

Then there is the electronic networking. Lois Weinstein has written about the value to information customers and staff alike of the various listservs available through the Internet, and of course the Internet offers a communications link to a multitude of library systems that have online public access catalogs, as well as OPACs with full-text databases (Weinstein, pp. 18–19). The recent excursion of the one-person library community into its own listserv, sponsored by the Solo Librarians Division of the Special Libraries Association, has proved to be a phenomenal success. In providing one-person librarians with direct connections to colleagues who work in similar situations, the listserv has opened networking opportunities that, for many, simply would not have existed. Just a brief review of the first few months of the listserv's operation yields a great number of exchanges, some trivial and some of major importance. One subscriber, for example, was seeking help with a cost–benefit analysis, because her library was faced with the possibility of becoming either a fee-based service or going on an allocation system. She needed to know how to develop a cost–benefit analysis or an algorithm for calculating how to charge for time and overhead, and the listserv gave her a forum. Other information exchanges have been equally rewarding, dealing with such subjects as the sharing of Internet addresses for job listings, sources for cheap online cataloging software, references to literature on specific subjects (particularly hard-to-find and 'gray' literature), the purchasing and leasing of library equipment and many other useful topics, including a series of messages on what makes a good library. An additional benefit to the sponsoring organization has been a noticeable growth in membership ('SLA's . . .,' pp. 1-3).

8.   *Preferring no hierarchy to a hierarchy.* There is considerable attention being given in management circles to eliminating or minimizing the hierarchical management structures that have traditionally been associated with libraries and information services management, and certainly the innovative information department is going to look at the structure and determine where it can be 'loosened up.' Some authorities recommend what is known as a 'flattened' structure, in which many layers are eliminated and employees are empowered to make decisions themselves, and others, like Paul Saffo at the Institute for the Future in Menlo Park, California, point out that more of our organization charts are beginning to look like webs, which he calls 'the quintessential biological structure' ('Hierarchy?' p. 4). Regardless of the 'style,' the entrepreneurial library works best when the managers and staff can think independently of organizational constraints, and, hopefully, the processes and products emanating from the library can be constantly improved.

One of the most remarkable indications that a manager is thinking outside the hierarchy is the commitment to customer services. Miriam A. Drake, Dean and Director of the Libraries and Information Center at the Georgia Institute of Technology in Atlanta, Georgia, has created a system that represents exactly that point of view. Created in 1985, the electronic delivery system was one of the first to make a catalog and leased databases available to all faculty and students on the campus-wide network. It was this system that began the transformation of the library from a collection-based entity to a customer-based one, and a customer focus continues to be Drake's primary interest. For example, she is concerned about dealing with the materials of the past. 'Much basic work was done in the past,' she says, 'and in fields such as civil engineering, for example, we need to be able to access the records of that work, not just as an historical archive, but as basic, foundation material which is and will continue to be referred to by practitioners in that field for a long time to come. But that doesn't mean we don't look for progress, that we don't move forward when we have the opportunity. That is part of the whole customer-driven focus. We have to recognize that even though we must prepare for the day when the Nintendo kids have completed their PhDs and are running our classrooms, we will continue to have customers who want to come to a library building to smell and touch the volumes' ('Mimi Drake . . .,' pp. 2-3). It is this kind of thinking, putting the customers first in the scheme, that exemplifies the best entrepreneurial thinking in information managers today.

9.   *Working alone (independent working style) vs working with others.* Entrepreneurial responsibility does not rest entirely upon senior management, as is being recognized in the literature:

> Although the important role of senior managers in creating an entrepreneurial climate is acknowledged . . . corporate entrepreneurship is both a top down and a bottom up process reliant on the initiatives emanating from below as much as on the creation of a receptive climate from above. (Ginsberg and Hay, p. 382)

There are, in fact, many information services providers who are able to bring an entrepreneurial perspective to their work, both people who work in single-staff situations or with others in a department but whose working style is primarily solo (or whose work is so distinctive that they in effect work alone). Such people have opportunities to be entrepreneurs and innovators simply because they see, at first hand, what the information customers are seeking and are frequently in a position – because of the special relationship that single-staff employees have with their customers – to cut through bureaucratic layers and provide the service instantaneously.

   An example can be found in a changed company policy about the purchasing of staff materials in a firm where, previously, the one-person librarian had purchased not only materials for the library but also certain materials for other staff. The new policy restricts library purchases to materials needed for the library itself, and any staff purchases must be handled through a central purchasing department. Rather than see this as a lost opportunity the librarian decided to assume an advisory or consulting role for staff before they went to the purchasing department. Doing this, she could continue to advise people about how look for materials to be ordered, how to deal with prices etc., and also show them how to provide the purchasing department with the exact information needed for an effective (and hopefully, fast) transaction. This librarian continued to be an interested party in helping the customers meet their information needs, and was not required to be involved in the actual orders themselves.

10.   *More risk taking vs risk aversion.* Few library leaders have as clear an understanding of the role of entrepreneurial thinking in library and information services as does Donald Riggs. In a well-known essay Riggs linked entrepreneurial thinking with strategic planning and managed to convey the importance of both to the library. Nevertheless, Riggs cautioned: '. . . strategic planning and entrepreneurship should not be perceived as cure-alls for library issues, but they can be described as means for the reassertion of an innovative climate in the library construct' (Riggs, p. 42).

For the information services unit attempting continuous improvement to service delivery, the incorporation of a new model or paradigm can be unsettling, unless there is an entrepreneurial framework to the place. This was certainly the case at BP Exploration in the late 1980s. John Wilson was working for BP then, and he began to think in terms of the librarian as an internal consultant, the professional information practitioner who can bring expertise and specific problem-solving ability to the company. If obtained externally these skills would be prohibitively expensive or, at the very least, difficult to justify. By training selected internal information professionals to refocus their efforts into a 'consultancy mode,' both the information operation and the parent organization benefit.

When Wilson explains his concept of internal consultancy, it becomes clear that one of the first requirements is an understanding - on the part of senior managers involved - of the various types of consultancy. Wilson has identified three, which he uses as he brings his internal consultancy model into the information organization:

● The direct purchase of information or expertise, in which the client has correctly diagnosed the problem, but does not have the skills, resources, or desire to provide a solution from within the organization.

● The doctor–patient model, which Wilson characterizes as something like this from the client: 'I know that there is something wrong, and I would like you to find out what it is and I want you to either tell me what to do or fix it.'

● The process consultation model, in which the client is aware of the problem, but not of its precise nature, or in which the client does not know what type of help is needed or what is available, or in which the client could benefit from being involved in the diagnosis of the problem.

In all three the running theme is that the information services staff - having the expertise - can act as consultants to solve the clients' problems. At the same time, management can see the justification, in terms of resource management, for using the information staff in this way.

11. More concerned with immediate vs long-term results. The best customer service is when staff are empowered to cut through bureaucratic layers and get the information to the customers in the format and manner that best meets their needs. Consider, for example, what happens when an architect, working for a city's planning commission on a restoration project in a historical quarter of the city, discovers that he needs to see the city directory for the years immediately before World War II. The only source for this material is the local history collection of the public library, where he is not only offered the material he needs, but is invited to have one of his staff come for the material and bring it back to his office, as long as it is returned to the public library by the next morning. At this public library, the staff have been trained in what the city's library director calls 'entrepreneurial information delivery' and all departments are encouraged to think about information requests from the point of view of the customer. Certainly losses could be irreparable, but on the other hand the material is not being used while it resides on the shelf, and most people needing a book of this type would not have the time to come to the library to use it. So even though there are rules about the use of materials from the special collections, in this case it made sense to 'bend the rules' and take a proactive approach to meet the user's needs. Obviously some borrowers are trustworthy and would understand the delicacy and importance of the material. Others, perhaps, not so well educated or trained might not be offered the same privilege. In both cases the entrepreneurial management approach permitted the staff member to make the decision about how the material would be used.

12. More integration vs more specialization. As we move deeper and deeper into the Information Age, the interest in 'one-stop shopping' for information customers becomes more and more apparent. Elizabeth Bole Eddison of Inmagic Inc. in the United States and Elizabeth Orna of The Orna/Stevens Consultancy in the United Kingdom have both been credited for their work – done separately – in recognizing that from the customer's point of view, the specialization and separation of information by format, type, subject or any other criterion is inefficient and leads, as often as not, to discouragement with the information delivery process. The information services field is looking to the integration of information as an important next step. In the meantime, the innovative information services manager works, as far as possible, with others in the organization to provide one-stop shopping wherever it is feasible and looks forward to the next generation of information technology whereby the customer will only need to ask for information in one place.

This is certainly a concept that Peter Emmerson at Barclays Bank has been thinking about. As head of Barclays Records Services since 1987, Emmerson has long been aware that an issue that comes up with some frequency is the need for information services to be more focused and more integrated, more related to one another. For example, as part of his responsibility Emmerson manages the bank's corporate records center, the largest in the UK, and it is a position which gives him the opportunity to look at the entire information spectrum at Barclays. From this perspective he can track how the company uses both internal and external information, and can see how the two types of information are connected (or not, as the case may be). Emmerson is not sure that all information staff understand the value of integrated information services.

Information 'warehousing' is built on a myth, he says, a myth that all information is equally valuable, so it becomes difficult to train staff to understand what should be retained and what should not. Internal information, of course, is more specific but is often only part of a larger need that includes external information gathered from elsewhere. To Emmerson's way of thinking, information staff must understand that the customer's needs might incorporate both types of information.

The logical extension of the integrated information concept is, of course, the information kiosk, where an information 'navigator' or 'consultant' is on duty to direct the inquirer to the appropriate resource or provide the information directly if possible. This approach represents one of the three 'layers' of the information services model that has been created at Cooper & Lybrand. As described by Patricia S. Foy, Cooper & Lybrand's Director of Libraries and Technology Research, these are:

> Desktop – providing access to basic business information either through the PC or the kiosk
>
> Information Fulfillment Center – a centralized 24-hour help desk
>
> Networked information specialists – providing the information that cannot easily be 'put into a database' or generated as a repetitive request. (Foy, p. 49)

In terms of entrepreneurial information delivery, it is C&L's kiosk effort that makes so much sense:

> The kiosk is tailored to 'high-voltage' and vertical industry-specific user groups, such as health care, telecommunications, and retail. It is self-contained and interactive and could include computers, CD-ROM, touchscreen, video, sound, or print capabilities. . . . The second tier will take place through an *information fulfillment center*. Repetitive, on-demand documents or information will be available 24 hours a day, essentially fulfilling 'anytime, anyplace' requirements. This access will include such capabilities as securities pricing; fact-checking; fax-on-demand; document, form, or publications delivery; and periodicals processing. In this tier, the routine, paraprofessional, or non-expert activities and functions, which comprised as much as 50% of skilled librarians' time, are being merged. In addition to providing a centralized, easy-to-reach facility, this center will enhance productivity and reduce costs. Purchasing and financial management will also be centralized and coordinated. Portions of this activity will be networked and some may be outsourced.
>
> The fulfillment center will provide 'information help desk' services such as the following types of activities:
>
> *   performs simple factual reference
> *   identifies sources and verifies references
> *   directs users to alternative service/product providers

* gathers and transmits research materials
* undertakes standard literature searches
* selectively disseminates information
* maintains databases of information
* controls the C&L catalog

(Foy, p. 50)

Working within the organization at large

In looking for continuous improvement, entrepreneurial managers often find themselves caught in a bind. For example, according to Paul Osterman, when people are asked to describe how information technology changes work, the discussion usually focuses on two questions: the impact of IT on the level of employment, and secondly, its impact on the content of particular occupations, such as skills and duties (Osterman, pp. 220 ff.). Not only must information services managers focus on the number of people required to deliver the information products, services and consultations, but these activities must be carried out with whatever organizational technology is in place. Such constraints often lead to conflicts with 'territorial' overtones.

These conflicts can be avoided by looking at several ideas, all to do with the organization and its institutional culture. Osterman notes that

**Link the change to
information policy
already in place**

**Take it "to the floor":
Will information customers
benefit from the change?**

Is it feasible in IT terms?

**What are the staff requirements
to implement the change?**

**Is there support *and* enthusiasm
from senior management?**

Figure 9.1   Selling entrepreneurial change in the information services environment

the impact of the technology in each area is 'contingent on context.' For the information services executive, specific productivity standards must be tracked and, where the installation of an electronic process can improve productivity or enhance a system already in place, data about the benefits must be gathered and analyzed. With this analysis in hand, managers can:

1. Link the new procedure, technique, or product to the organization's information policy. The information staff and senior management will have already agreed on the policy.

2. Take the idea to 'the floor,' that is, determine whether information customers will truly benefit from the adoption of the new procedure, product or service.

3. Determine from MIS staff whether the product is feasible, both financially and from a support perspective.

4. Project staff levels for the delivery of the information product or service in question.

5. Establish support from senior management.

Working with others in the organization, information services managers have plenty of opportunities to introduce innovation, but they must plan their strategy carefully. If the improved product or service is going to be accepted, it must be connected to the larger organizational picture and the larger organizational success (Figure 9.1).

References

Barrier, Michael. 'Small firms put quality first.' *Nation's Business*, 80 (5), May, 1992.

Carrier, Camille. 'Intrapreneurship in large firms and SMRs: a comparative study.' *International Small Business Journal*, 12 (3), April–June, 1994.

Champion, Brian. 'Intrapreneuring and the spirit of innovation in libraries.' *Journal of Library Administration*, 9 (2), 1988.

Duston, Beth. 'The fugitive user.' *The One-Person Library: A Newsletter for Librarians and Management*, 10 (2), June, 1993.

Foy, Patricia S. 'The re-invention of the corporate information model – the information professional's role in empowering today's workforce.' *The Power of Information: Transforming the World/Professional Papers from the 86th Annual Conference of the Special Libraries Association, June 10–15, 1995, Montréal, Quebec, Canada.* Washington DC: Special Libraries Association, 1995.

Ginsberg, Ari, and Hay Michael, 'Confronting the challenges of corporate entrepreneurship: guidelines for venture managers.' *European Management Journal*, 12 (4), December, 1994.

'Hierarchy? Flat? Or *Web*? What's Your Management Style?' *InfoManage: The International Management Newsletter for the Information Services Executive*, 2 (7), June, 1995.

Lau, Theresa and Chan, K.F. 'The incident method: an alternative way of studying entrepreneurial behavior.' *Irish Business and Administrative Research*, 15, 1994.

'Mimi Drake at Georgia Tech: Ten Years Online and The Future is NOW!' *InfoManage: The International Management Newsletter for the Information Services Executive*, 2 (6), May, 1995.

Osterman, Paul. 'The impact of IT on jobs and skills.' *The Corporation of the 1990s: Information Technology and Organizational Transformation*. Michael S. Scott Morton, ed. New York: Oxford University Press, 1991.

Pinchot, Gifford III. *Intrapreneuring: Why You Don't Have to Leave the Corporation to Become an Entrepreneur*. New York: Harper & Row, 1985.

Riggs, Donald E. 'Entrepreneurial spirit in strategic planning.' *Journal of Library Administration*, 8 (1), Spring, 1987.

'SLA's solo librarians now online: solos' Internet listserv a smashing success.' *The One-Person Library: A Newsletter for Librarians and Management*, 12 (4), August, 1995.

Weinstein, Lois. 'LIFENET/INTERNET and the health science librarian.' *Special Libraries*, 85 (1), Winter, 1994.

Chapter Ten

When it doesn't work: dealing with the downside

Flexibility and adaptability are required characteristics in any managerial position, and providing entrepreneurial management for a library or other information services operation is no exception. There are going to be times when even the best of ideas don't work out, or aren't accepted by those in authority, and when this happens the entrepreneurial manager looks at what went wrong, tries to figure out how to avoid it happening again, and moves forward with another version of what he or she is attempting to achieve. Broadly speaking, most 'failures' fall into one of three categories: those in which organizational compromises must be made; those in which professional concessions must be made; and those in which personal disappointments must be dealt with. In all three the negative feelings come not so much from a sense of failure but from the emotional investment that the entrepreneurial manager and his or her staff have in the success of the department and its work.

'Emotional investment' is not a bad thing, and for most professionals it is this that distinguishes them from non-professionals. In our society we have long encouraged workers to commit themselves to their work, to enjoy what they are doing, and to arrange their lives so that they look forward to coming in to work each day. These are simplistic values, but they very specifically define for many of us what we mean when we talk about our work: it is something we like, we're glad we're doing it, and apart from the security and the compensation, there are real feelings of accomplishment connected with working in the information services field. So when one accepts that one has an emotional investment in one's work it simply means that the employee recognizes that his job is important and through it he is making a contribution to his organization and, presumably, to society at large.

So when an entrepreneurial effort fails an emotional response is appropriate: no-one ever tries to accomplish something without being disappointed when it fails. At the same time, however, the disappointed entrepreneur thinks about what went wrong, looks for the places where wrong decisions were made, and moves forward to the next challenge. That is what life is all about.

Organizational compromises

While there are times when it seems appropriate to look for a specific individual to blame, sometimes failure is nothing more than the result of an organizational or corporate culture that is not ready for a change being proposed. Think, for example, about the librarian who has management responsibility for a research library and archives for a small landscape architectural firm on the west coast of Florida. There the library has four staff, and the work is done well. The scientists and engineers in the firm (the library supports an operation of about 40 people) rely on the library staff for research information, there is a considerable amount of literature searching using various databases, and the organization's archives, project files and similar documents are kept in good order.

There is a problem in the company, however, and the librarian – thinking entrepreneurially – determines to do what she can to fix it. She has noticed that there is a great deal of waste and inefficiency in the way information is handled. It's all done very amateurishly, and the librarian knows that many people in the organization – her own staff included – would appreciate some consistency in the way information decisions are made. Much effort is expended in obtaining customer files, for example, and connecting these to plans and reports requires much energy and is not accomplished without considerable frustration, since the plans and reports are stored in various places (some in the library, some in the file room, some offsite). Other records (human resources, marketing etc.) are well organized, but none of the departments and offices where they are kept are connected, so no-one really knows who has what records.

However, the information problems are not taken very seriously, but improvements could still be made. In fact, the librarian has discovered a 'template' information policy that would be perfect for this company. Very little additional work would have to be done to bring the policy in line with how business is done at the firm, and the model seems almost to have been designed with this company in mind. So the librarian set out to try and organize a company-wide information policy.

This entrepreneurial librarian did all the right things: first she talked about the idea with her own staff, and everyone agreed that it should be pursued. The next step was to put the idea on the agenda for the twice-weekly management meeting. The librarian produced a short explanatory document and distributed it to the other managers who would be attending the meeting. At the meeting everyone seemed to think the idea was a good one, and the company president asked the librarian, the head of the computer services department and his own administrative assistant to form a task force to study its feasibility.

The task force met a couple of times, and while the librarian had the sense that the president's administrative assistant liked the idea of an information policy, the manager of computer services was not enthusiastic. He was mildly hostile to the concept and not at all sure he wanted his department to be interfered with (which was how he interpreted the idea, since he considered that anything to do with 'information' was his domain, and he did not appreciate having the librarian bring this idea to the table). Nevertheless, the task force reported to the managers at the next meeting that they had discussed the idea and were willing to have discussions continue. The computer services manager made it clear, however, that he was much too busy to be involved, and the task force would only be able to meet when he could fit the meetings into his busy schedule.

Now the president got into the act. As he and other managers had discussed the idea with other employees (and in a couple of cases with key customers and one or two suppliers with whom the company had fairly close business relationships), the idea seemed more and more like a good one and several people, including some of the scientists and engineers, asked to be added to the task force. By the end of the meeting the task force numbered twelve, including the president and one of the suppliers, and the librarian found herself taking the chair. Since she knew this would provide her with good exposure as well as identify her as one of the 'movers and shakers' in the company, she did not object.

The project got out of hand. Within a very short time the librarian and her assistant were spending inordinate amounts of time organizing meetings, preparing agendas and dealing with meetings that the head of computer services would have to cancel at the last minute. Within a few weeks, the task force had met only once, the company's busiest work season was beginning and it soon became clear that no further work could be done until later in the year. Further meetings were planned, then cancelled. Finally, after about a year of frustration, it became clear to the librarian that the task force was not going to be able to do its work. The idea seemed to fade away, no-one missed it, and no-one brought it up. Even the president never mentioned it again, and the company continued with its informal policy, which seemed sufficient. There development and implementation of an information policy was not characterized as vital to the successful growth of the firm, so the idea simply withered away.

What happened? Is there an explanation for why such a good idea should fail? When an entrepreneurial manager proposes an idea, it should be picked up and at least taken to some experimental or testing stage that would provide feedback as to whether or not it is, in fact, a good idea.

In this case several influential forces were at play, and describing them can provide guidelines for what the entrepreneurial librarian should do when organizational compromises must be reached. As an entrepreneurial idea begins to bloom, the following questions should be asked:

1.   What is the political landscape in the organization? Is an entrepreneurial/innovative approach to organizational issues welcome? It was not a mistake for this librarian to assume that she could bring the idea of an information policy to the company successfully. It is an innovative company, it is successful, and the general ambience is one of moving forward. Furthermore, by bringing the suggestion to her own staff first she was able to get a 'reading' from the people with whom she worked most closely, who were also the people who most understood the role of information delivery for their various customers. So the entrepreneurial idea passed its first test.

Thought might have been given to one political consideration, however, i.e. the *way* in which innovative change moved through the organization. Judging from subsequent events it would seem that the librarian would have been wise to identify other changes that had recently been incorporated into the company's operations and have given some attention to how they had been brought forward, who had worked on them, who advocated them and who opposed them, and so forth. Having done so, she might have discovered trends and points of view that would have been useful to her as she proposed her idea. The president, for example, might be a man of great initial enthusiasms but not interested in long-term projects. Or there might be other people in the company who ostensibly aren't characterized as 'movers and shakers' but who have a great deal of influence. If there are such people, they need to be identified and brought into the movement for change, as advocates.

2. What will be the benefits of incorporating this activity into the workplace? It seemed clear to the librarian that there was enough frustration to justify efforts to improve the situation. That was her informed opinion and the people she sought as advisers – her own staff – would naturally agree with her. However, this frustration was not enough of an incentive to propel the activity forward. Prior to meeting with her own staff, the librarian would have been well advised to have met with other department heads to establish that they, too, felt that the information flow was subject to enough hindrances to make it worthwhile pursuing a firm-wide information policy. In doing so the librarian would not only have been setting the stage for a more positive reception of her idea, but would have been creating interest among the information stakeholders.

3.   Are there any staff members who will not support this activity? Why? Early on in her own deliberations the librarian should have looked over the firm's various departments, thinking about the people in those departments and how they use information, and put together an impression of how they might feel about changing the way information is moved through the company. That there would be interest in the matter quickly became apparent when the subject was first brought up; having so many people volunteer to serve on the task force meant that there were many people in the organization who are interested in information. These people should have been thought about, and if they were likely to oppose the idea this should have been identified.

Ideally, of course, this kind of information comes forth when an information audit is performed, which should have been the first step. By taking the project to the management meeting before an audit could be arranged, the librarian was restricted to *estimating* what the political landscape was, and that was not good enough.

4.　*Can the development of this activity be incorporated into the current work schedule? Is additional staffing required?* While funding for special projects is not especially difficult to obtain in this particular organization, the librarian's innocence seriously inhibited her own enthusiasm once the study began. Again, a quiet talk with a senior manager might have alleviated some of the stress in the librarian's own department, for a more experienced person would have recognized that help would be needed and offered to provide such help.

5.　*What resources are required for the development of this activity? How much time, money and staff will be used in the various stages of its progress?* Similarly, the informal description of the idea should have raised questions about support for such a project. In any enterprise of this nature the organization has some experience, and reasonable predictions about the amount of support required could be made. More attention to this matter might have prevented some of the later problems. If additional staff, say, had been hired to coordinate the project, or if an external consultant had been brought in to facilitate the task force meetings and to make recommendations as the project progressed, interest would have been sustained.

6.　*Is there sufficient interest in the activity to justify the expenditure of resources?* Do people care? In this situation this is a very real question, for it is apparent that no-one in authority seems to connect the lack of an information policy with the company's business success. In fact, from the point of view of most of the information stakeholders the company is doing very well, thank you, and if there isn't a *need* to change the policy (or implement one) there is going to be very little enthusiasm for the idea.

7.   *Is there sufficient talent (competency) to ensure that the development of this activity is done properly? Should its development be outsourced?* If the idea is allowed to die as the organization gears up for its busy season, it is obvious that enthusiasm is not very high. Even so, if there is some enthusiasm consideration might be given to bringing in an external consultant to help to ensure that the information audit is conducted properly and adequately, that the project stays on track, and that the information stakeholders are all trained to implement the policy once it is in place. Organizing a project of this magnitude and expecting it to be 'folded in' to the usual working patterns of the librarian and the other members of the task force is naïve and leaves the entire proposal open to being characterized as frivolous (Figure 10.1).

These, then, are the questions that must be asked by anyone seeking to put forward an entrepreneurial idea. They are not meant to discourage, but to temper the enthusiasm of the innovator with a mild dose of organizational realism. Answering these questions enables the entre-

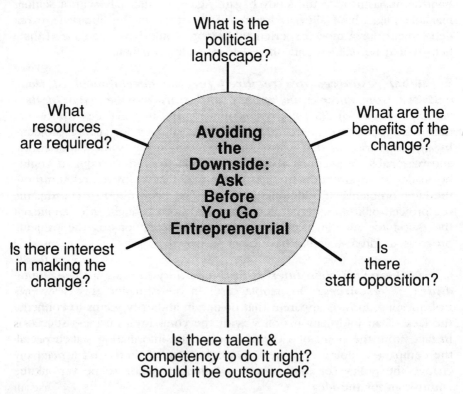

Figure 10.1

preneurial librarian to prepare herself for her next effort, and if she is wise she will use the experience to make a better attempt when another idea comes to her. What she does not do is 'cave in' because this particular innovation did not succeed. At this point in the company's history the corporate culture did not lend itself to this specific change, but that does not mean the organization would frown on all change. In fact, now that the ice has been broken with respect to a firm-wide information policy it is quite possible that the subject will come up again, at which time the librarian and her staff will be ready. In the meantime, they look for other information innovations they can bring to the company.

Professional concessions

The emphasis throughout this book has been on the high standards of information delivery that are expected in an entrepreneurial library. All librarians and information services employees should have the highest standards of performance for their work, and are naturally very disappointed when their entrepreneurial efforts fail. They have put their professional values on the line, and when they are rejected, or are not equal to the challenge with which they have been presented, there is a sense of 'failing one's profession'.

An example of such a situation occurred not long ago in a large engineering consulting firm in Texas. The research library is a major resource for the company, many of whose civil engineering projects – bridges, roadways, and so forth – are government contracts. The library staff consists of thirty-five employees, of which nineteen are professionally trained and have graduate degrees in library and/or information studies. Because the company has been very successful in the last two years in acquiring several high-profile projects, and because some of these projects will be relatively long-term multimillion-dollar undertakings, the firm's library director has been meeting with other managers to work out how additional professional staffing will be brought in to handle the additional work. The group has come up with several recommendations, and the management committee that has approval authority has been totally willing, with one exception, to go along with all them. The exception is that for the research library, which will be acquiring three new professional information employees as well as three new support staff, the management committee has rejected the idea of graduate librarians for the three professional positions and is instead requiring subject specialists with, preferably, some information background. In effect, the company is looking at a new hiring policy that will bring civil engineers into the information field, and the present situation is being used to ease in the new policy. The library director doesn't like the idea, but as a member of the management team looking at overall hiring practices he has accepted it and must now present it to the library staff.

The attempt in the earlier example to develop a firm-wide information policy required that organizational compromises be made; this move to staff a research facility with subject specialists instead of librarians requires professional concessions. Again, questions can be asked:

1.   Is the firm unwilling to hire subject specialists who are also trained librarians? Initial enquiries have determined that trained librarians who are also subject specialists in civil engineering are scarce. Since so few candidates with both qualifications are available, the company has looked at its customer service requirements and concluded that what is needed is a familiarity with the literature and with the type of work the firm does. It is the opinion of the management committee that subject specialists will better understand the needs of the information customers in the firm, and that such employees could master the philosophical and technical requirements of librarianship through on-the-job training. The library director has recognized the validity of this point of view, but he has pointed out that the learning curve for these employees will be longer than if they were librarians, especially librarians with a scientific background. Nevertheless, since the committee has ruled that the new positions be filled in this manner the library director has agreed to do so, and is doing his best to distance himself from his disappointment.

2.   What is the level of service the subject specialists will be capable of delivering? Who will the information customers be? Information audits over the course of several years have determined that members of the engineering staff are frequently frustrated with the level of service they receive from the company library. Although the staff are willing to provide them with what they need, they are frequently called into what the library staff refer to as 'information consultations', to discuss how the engineers can advise the librarians so that they can fill their information requests. However, the professional librarians are frequently unable to provide the level of information the engineers need, resulting in disappointment for the engineers and frustration for the librarians, who are aware that they are not as expert with these queries as they would like to be.

3.   How will the subject specialists be trained in information delivery? The library director is aware that the lack of technical expertise in librarianship will slow the new employees' entrance into the company as mainstream information providers, but he expects this to be offset by the goodwill and subject expertise that will be shared with the present team of graduate librarians. The director has realigned the job description of one of his direct subordinates to include a training component, and this person will supervise the organization of team training workshops so that current staff will be working closely with the new subject specialists. The goal, of course, is that there will be a leveling off of expertise, with the librarians sharing their information philosophy and technical skills with the subject specialists, and the subject specialists sharing their expertise with the librarians.

4.What is the expected effect on library staff morale? The library director and his assistant have discussed the morale issue on a number of occasions, and have decided that the best way to deal with the situation is to explain to the professional staff why this decision has been made. Little direct resistance is expected and a particular point of their presentation to the professional staff will be to emphasize that, as employees, they have a first loyalty to the company, which takes precedence over their loyalty to the profession. The director and his assistant also plan to make it clear that they are in agreement with the decision: it is not their practice to accept a decision and then to disparage it when it is implemented.

Personal disappointments

In almost every entrepreneurial situation in which the innovation is not permitted to thrive, the person who owns the idea suffers personal disappointment.

In a large scientific institute affiliated with a major university on the west coast, one of the most important parts of the library's collection is the complete set of the institute's research publications, published by the university press. The library maintains both bound copies and 'file' copies, and these materials are heavily used by the institute's staff, by university faculty and graduate students, by visiting scholars, and occasionally by the general public. Through an arrangement with the university press, sales of individual research reports are handled through the library. It's not an onerous task, and it's a fairly straightforward process: when requests come in one of the staff photocopies the file copy and sends it on to the buyer. The invoice is copied to the university press, which collects the payment and keeps it.

The staff member who works with this material came up with the idea that the publications should be available in CD-ROM format, and that income from the sales of the CD-ROM product should be used to support the library. The librarian asked the employee to write up the suggestion, which would then be passed on to the institute's director. This was done; the librarian was full of praise for the employee, and fully expected to be able to pass on some sort of bonus to her for her good suggestion.

As it turned out, the plan backfired. The institute's Executive Board and the university press did indeed decide to transfer the publications to CD-ROM, and the hard copy of the publications was transferred to offsite storage. But the income from the sale of the CD-ROM products did not come back to the library, and now the staff are continually frustrated because so many people want the hard copies and are still coming to the library for them, only to be told that they are no longer available.

In advising the employee, the librarian must be careful not to inhibit future innovative thinking, and the point must be made that the decision to change the components of the original recommendations should in no way alter the positive reinforcement that is provided. The employee did a good job and was thinking of how it could be done better when she made her suggestion, and she had no idea that it would be used in such a way that the library itself would suffer.

In a situation such as this, the manager has to determine the context of the disappointment. Did the entrepreneurial employee have a *personal* stake in the acceptance of her innovation? Was her work and that of her colleagues going to be seriously hampered because the innovation did not succeed, or because the situation did not turn out the way it had been expected to? It is the role of the entrepreneurial information services manager to see that the employee is not discouraged from putting forth other ideas, and to see that the entire staff benefits from knowing that, even when entrepreneurial ideas do not work out, they are not necessarily bad ideas because they were different.

Chapter Eleven

(with Beth Duston)

The tangible payoffs: making a profit from the organization's investment in information services

Much attention is being given to the 'information age', and there are those who contend that our society has evolved from the industrial society of the late nineteenth and early twentieth centuries directly into an age wherein information is the key to success, whatever the endeavor. Not quite. Information has always been the key, even in the heyday of manufacturing, but the conveying of information, the seeking, storing, retrieval and dissemination of that information, was not as sophisticated as it is today. In any case, in the days of the Industrial Revolution and the years that followed, the handling of information was personal and involved one-on-one contact between the information users and the information handlers unless they were one and the same.

Now we have matured into a service society, and with the growth of sophisticated communications technology it is only natural that information handling has become an essential. And information technology, being made up of so many diverse components, each lending itself to private and profitable cooperation and distribution, lends itself equally to the entrepreneurial motive. Indeed, as far as information technology is concerned we are at the very center of an entrepreneurial bonanza in the buying and selling of information and of the sophisticated links which are required for its adequate dissemination.

Never has there been a time for individual entrepreneurism such as the present. Entrepreneurs are now a part of our society: they are now so numerous and so influential – and command so much respect – that the entire 'tone' of society has reversed itself and the entrepreneurial course is approved, emulated and encouraged. Only a couple of generations back such societal acceptance was not the norm, and to think entrepreneurially was to be a little 'different.' This is no longer the case. And in the information services field, as communications technology has become more and more sophisticated, more and more specialists have appeared, each of them skilled and able to support one angle, to appeal to one niche market, to participate in one particular aspect of 'the information society.' These information entrepreneurs are literally changing the world.

The librarian as intrapreneur

There is naturally a great deal of appeal for librarians and other information specialists to look at the information marketplace and think about how the services and products they provide might be offered to a broader audience. Certainly the entrepreneurial library manager takes advantage of entrepreneurial skills to bring new information products to his or her users, and to organize the functions of the library so that innovative thinking can prevail. If this is what the librarian can do for his or her constituent market, cannot these same successes be offered to customers beyond the specified boundaries of the information services operation with which he or she is associated? Can the librarian succeed in this market-driven role? The answer depends, of course, on the personal and professional characteristics of the librarian. Success as an entrepreneur/intrapreneur calls for specific character traits, most of which have now been enumerated.

In thinking about these matters, a broader definition now exists:

> . . . intrapreneurship is defined as the taking in charge of an innovation by an employee or other individual working under the control of an enterprise. Innovation in this context means the introduction of a change leading to an increase in the firm's competitiveness. (Carrier, p. 60)

The definition builds, of course, on the work of Gifford Pinchot, who has studied the intrapreneurial concept for several years and to whom is given credit for bringing the idea before the corporate world. The term is Pinchot's trademarked label for 'intracorporate entrepreneurship' (Hartman, p. 69). For the rest of us, it identifies the activity when we take something we're doing and come up with the vision to market it outside the immediate organization for which it was created, for a profit. Pinchot is basically referring to products and services developed within the corporate setting through the vision and enthusiasm of people who would be entrepreneurs if they were not part of the corporate structure. The key word here is 'vision,' for all entrepreneurs and intrapreneurs share this common characteristic: they are visionary, and they 'ride to the discovery of successful ventures on the strength of their vision' (Pinchot, 1985, p. 37). Other important concepts are of course very similar to those described earlier when we looked at the entrepreneurial mindset in general, except that in the context of intrapreneurism these characteristics - things like innovation, persistence, flexibility, enthusiasm, and a serious and enthusiastic working relationship with a sponsor -

relate very specifically to the development of a profitable return for the organization and not for the individual.

There are, indeed, information services professionals who have these characteristics. Not all of them, of course, and some are more visionary than others, just as some are more innovative or persistent than others. Nevertheless, there are those who can take these attributes and come up with information products and services that can bring profit to the organization. Some have been very successful at it. They didn't do it on their own: they had the ideas – or cooperated with others who had the ideas and together they made things happen. And while the same phenomenon is taking place to some extent in public and academic libraries, by and large the primary locus of successful intrapreneurial information services seems to be in the specialized library field (probably because a certain amount of entrepreneurial thinking is required just to keep one's job).

As noted earlier, it was Sylvia Piggott who pointed out that businesses and professions are reengineering and restructuring as a consequence of the exponential leap in information technology. This enabling technology will, Piggott believes, lead to vast improvements in customer-valued productivity, optimization of businesses, and competitiveness. Certainly in the specialized library field Piggott's assertions are coming true, for specialized librarians can now use information technology not only to acquire, process and disseminate information for their customers, but can also produce information both for their own customers and for customers beyond their own sphere, a truly intrapreneurial activity. Nearly all specialized librarians are giving some thought to doing this, particularly in the larger organizations. Many are succeeding very well, and nowadays it is not at all unusual for a company library to gather information for its internal customers and then turn that information – in a different format – into products that can be marketed to other customers. It is the wave of the future.

Certainly Paul Davenport's important work on process innovation has contributed much toward moving information services management in this direction, for it is in the analysis of workflow processes that such ideas come to the innovators. Davenport offers five 'key activities' for identifying processes which might be candidates for innovation:

- identify major processes
- determine process boundaries
- assess strategic relevance of each process
- render high-level judgments of the 'health' of each process
- qualify the culture and politics of each process

(Davenport, p. 27)

The directions on this list lead almost inevitably to a sixth 'key activity,' which would be to determine how an information-related process can be manipulated so that the product that results from its implementation can be disseminated to a broader audience than originally sought it.

Requirements for intrapreneurial success

The specific critical components in the intrapreneurial process have been identified by Judy Macfarlane, who is the Director of the Business Information Center in the Montréal office of Price Waterhouse. When Macfarlane came to the company in early 1994, she had a specific job to do. She was to design and implement a Business Information Center and she was to do it in three years. It would be a challenge, for there had been no central information resource for the Montréal office until she appeared on the scene. But Macfarlane was undaunted by the task: it was something she knew she could do, and she knew she would do it well, and she threw herself into her work.

'The mandate was clear,' Macfarlane said in an interview. 'Price Waterhouse is a client-centered organization, and building up a business information resource as one of the services the company can offer to its clients makes a lot of sense. The firm's clients need this information and we're already providing it for our internal customers, so it's only appropriate that we structure our business information operation so that we can offer these services to our clients as well.'

According to Macfarlane, there are specific steps in the evolvement of an intrapreneurial business. 'Building the information infrastructure is the first part of the process,' she said. 'Once we agreed that the offering of business information services was a viable goal for Price Waterhouse, we stepped right in to planning and organizing the information operation so that it could be done. And to move in that direction, we had to first build the 'inside' infrastructure, to create a Business Information Center that would provide the information that the firm's staff needed in order to do its work.'

Obviously the strength of the information infrastructure is vital to the intrapreneurial effort, but at Price Waterhouse, it was a case of building an infrastructure from scratch. For many information services professionals the infrastructure is already in place and where they must be careful is in determining that the quality of the information products, services and consultations they provide for their internal customers is sufficiently good to offer to the external customers. Addressing this issue means that the products, services and consultations are reviewed and, if necessary, enhanced for the benefit of all information stakeholders. And the authority for this enhancement is senior management, a point that Judy Macfarlane made in the interview.

'The success of the intrapreneuring effort is built on commitment,' she said, 'commitment from the partners and commitment from the information staff. In fact, it's the commitment from the partners that is the second critical component of this operation. While we must first build up an internal information infrastructure, so that the partners and employees of Price Waterhouse have available to them the information services they need to do the work they must do, we must also have strong support from the partnership and that, I'm happy to say, is there.'

'Of course,' Macfarlane continued, 'the proof is in the success of the operation. You have to remember that any success in the accounting field

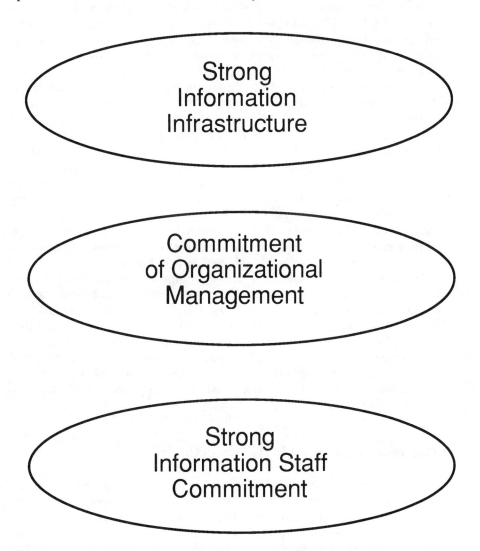

Figure 11.1   The keys to intrapreneurial success

Adapted from Judy A. Macfarlane, June, 1995

relates to the basis of the organization. We're a firm that earns its revenue from hourly charges to the client, and my staff and I – just like other Price Waterhouse employees – are required to file a specified number of chargeable hours per client. With internal customers, we charge against the accounts they are working for, and with external clients, we bill directly. In either case, it is a structure for evaluating – with a monetary value – the work we do.'

In those terms, just a few months short of the half-way mark in the start-up phase, the Business Information Center had been determined to be successful, and it had been a risk obviously worth taking. It had paid off. By that half-way point, the Business Information Center was already recovering fifty percent of the operational costs, and Macfarlane expected to double the number of external clients within another year.

The third component in this information picture is the commitment of the information staff, and that is where Macfarlane is particularly proud of the success of the operation. There are four of them in the Business Information Center, three information professionals and one support person. In addition to their work with external clients, the information team provides for the information needs of some 320 employees in the Montréal office and 75 or so at Quebec City. It's a big market and the workload is a full one, but no-one complains because all members of the information staff understand what their roles are. The team approach to information delivery – the value of which is one of Macfarlane's strong guiding principles – is implemented every day at the Business Information Center. It makes a lot of sense (Macfarlane, p. 1 ff.).

These three critical elements, the building of a strong internal information infrastructure, a commitment by senior management, and a commitment from information staff, are of course what make an intrapreneurial effort like the one at Price Waterhouse such a success. What they do, in effect, is combine with the basics of quality service such things as commitment to the customer, continuous improvement and the application of trust and teamwork in the information environment, to produce information products, and services that also enable the outside world to have access to them (Figure 11.1).

The relationship with the sponsor

The single most important component for the successful intrapreneuring of information products is the relationship with the sponsor. It is the enthusiastic support and commitment of senior management that will determine the success of the effort. Why is this? Because no innovative effort can exist in a vacuum. When an entrepreneurial manager brings forward ideas that can have a recognizable benefit to the parent organization, management is going to be interested.

Libraries and information centers have traditionally been considered financial liabilities for the organizations they serve. They are not expected to be profitable or even to be cost-effective. A study of the value of the corporate librarian and the information services he provides points out that 'information professionals are perceived to consume resources rather than generate revenue; their work cannot easily be apportioned and attributed to the unit cost of an industry's output' (Veaner, 1987). The same report goes on to offer reasons why information services are frequently not appreciated, and among the reasons listed is the fact that, traditionally, 'library products and services have been given away.' No-one – customer, researcher or manager – is going to appreciate something that comes free Is this, perhaps, an explanation why some libraries, especially those in the more traditional, non-corporate settings, are taken for granted?

Despite the role the information provided by the corporate library plays in the successful realization of the organizational mission, the possibility, however remote, of making money from the library is one that management is not trained to consider, and the innovative librarian or manager who can focus on the library or information center as a financial asset is well on the way to achieving a new and unique level of success. No longer will the library be a liability, draining resources from the company: it will be a productive profit center, contributing to the corporation's wellbeing.

Management views information in a variety of ways: in a competitive business, obviously, it is expected to give the company an edge over others in the same business. In services companies, the information is expected to result in better, more useful services (often described in terms of speed of delivery) for clients. Within the corporation the various departments determine their own information needs, depending on how their employees will use the information, and each department feeds its requirements into the corporate library for fulfillment. As the company grows, it is not unusual for a department's research programs to be separated from the corporate library, often to the extent of setting up a departmental library. Thus, within one organization, in addition to what might be called the 'corporate library,' there can be a marketing library, a product development library, a financial library, and even a personnel and human resources library. All of these exist to serve the corporate mission, and each of them is a potential resource for intrapreneuring services.

For the manager interested in what is going on in the library or information center, the librarian is a natural ally, for she already knows the role of the library in the organization. She has contact with the outside world and this contact is relatively objective. She knows what is going on not only in the library and information services field, but in the marketplace as well, for in order to do her work properly she must know her organization's place in the market and its place in whatever industry or service it represents. For her manager she is non-threatening, because she is not interested in becoming a manager herself. She is interested in the management of information and how it can be profitably used to support the corporate mission, and it is this attitude that which can be the basis of intrapreneurial success.

The corporate investment in information is not small, and even when we don't count the costs for the services, say, of a Chief Information Officer in the management line and the costs for the data-processing people in the support line, we are still left with a very large outlay of corporate funds. Money is spent on acquiring information, processing it, storing it and disseminating it. Time is expended by employees to do these things, and that time has a price attached to it. And both time and money relate to the determination of the value of information, for to an organization the value of information is based on the profit that derives from its use. In the Special Libraries Association Task Force Report referred to earlier, Miriam A. Drake quotes a King Research report which described how information services are valued: 'The value of library services can be assessed from three perspectives: what users are willing to pay (in terms of their time and effort) for information provided by the library, how much more it would cost them to use alternative sources for obtaining the information, and what benefits (or research costs avoidance) would be lost if the library did not exist' (King, 1987).

Winning sponsors to the cause

Ideally, senior managers and others of influence within the organization will be receptive to intrapreneurial innovations because they will contribute to the financial success of the organization. But if management doesn't hear about the good ideas through the normal scheme of things their support must be carefully sought, and this means that the entrepreneurial librarian must seek specific avenues for bringing ideas to the attention of those in authority. One tried and trusted way, of course, is to identify information products and services that managers themselves use and find out whether there are others who could use these same products and services. Another way is to look at certain products and services that management are acquiring externally and then determine how they might be provided from within the organization – with specific adaptations to make them of particular use and value to senior management – and then, if successful, marketed externally.

The best approach, of course, is to look at the idea, identify how the product or service supports internal customers, organize some basic market research with potential external customers, and then come up with a plan and deliver it to management with a request to discuss the idea. If it is a good idea and the potential profit is large enough to warrant the effort involved, management will recognize this and encourage the librarian to move forward.

It should be recognized that the achievement of managerial support is not always so structured, and many successful intrapreneurs in the information services field have pointed out that serendipity played a large part in their finding the management support they needed. Sometimes it just happens. Certainly that is what happened with a specialized librarian of our acquaintance. When a corporate officer was showing a visiting client through the firm's research operation, the librarian was simply asked if the company would do online searches for the client. The librarian made a noncommittal response, but thought about the request and brought the subject up with her manager later. The manager listened carefully when the librarian explained that the request was a workable one. Negotiations with the client were quickly completed and the firm found itself intrapreneuring its services. At a profit.

Regardless of how management support is achieved, there are basic questions to be asked, both by management and by the librarian. First, it has to be established whether they can work as a team. Teamwork in such an endeavor must be of the highest, most mutually supportive order. To put forward a change which goes so squarely against the mold as does intrapreneurial activity in an information environment is definitely a public relations risk, and each party must be able and willing to support the other.

Other questions have to do with the corporate or organizational culture. Is the corporate environment one in which the 'selling' of library services would be accepted? Or is the firm a more traditional organization in which the library is thought of as an established service, providing information without charge? What about the staff in the organization? If, for example, the library is part of a research and development unit, would the other members of the department – the 'primary' market, as it were – be comfortable with the idea of information services being offered to outsiders for a fee? Are levels of services to be equalized? Are external customers, billed directly, given exactly the same levels of service that internal customers are given, even though the chargebacks for the internal customers are charged to their clients? If so, how is this type of service monitored? These are the kinds of questions which must be asked, and the answers will determine whether or not the organization will support intrapreneurialism.

One way to determine whether intrapreneurial efforts are appropriate or not is to look at the size of the organization. Conventional wisdom would seem to be that intrapreneuring works best in smaller companies, or large companies in which the impersonal largeness has been alleviated by managerial efforts to encourage smaller departmental units. 'Many smaller companies today also have superb teams of specialists, and it is their concentration in the smaller company which can make fruitful partnering so rewarding for both sizes' (Landau, p. 22). In the smaller company, or a small department of a large corporation, the librarian is often the center of activity simply because she is the resource to which everyone turns for information. She can see the way things work in the company and because of her contacts with the outside world she knows which data and which techniques can be sold for a profit. She is the logical source for intrapreneurial products, if she has a supportive team to work with. And it is in the small company that she can provide this kind of innovation. Why? Because she provides what Landau calls 'focus . . . because small companies are often a more efficient instrument to get things done'.

The products

There is, of course, the question of whether the data and the techniques which can be offered in an intrapreneuring venture can be marketed, and it is here again where teamwork plays an important role. Most of what comes out of an information services unit is intangible (we are not talking about library-specific techniques, such as internally developed library software programs, for example: such products are tangible and present a different set of questions) and there are certain considerations that must be given to their marketing. For example, information is a very *finite* product. Once it has been received by the person requiring it, a particular piece of information or data is no longer necessary and, as such, it loses its value almost immediately. Therefore, the intrapreneuring librarian and her manager must look for marketing techniques, some of which were described in an article by Theodore Levitt:

> The product will be judged in part by who offers it – not just who the vendor corporation is but also who the corporation's representative is. The vendor and the vendor's representative are both inextricably and inevitably part of the 'product' that prospects must judge before they buy. The less tangible the generic product, the more powerfully and persistently the judgment about it gets shaped by the packaging – how it's presented, who presents it, and what's implied by metaphor, simile, symbol, and other surrogates for reality.
>
> (Levitt, p. 97)

Here is where the librarian and her managers exploit the historical perceptions of librarianship, the value of the librarian's service, the quality of the products and services associated with the library, and so on, for it is the reputation and integrity of the librarian that will be a major factor in the marketing of the intangible information product. The customers will want the products and services because of where they come from and who is associated with them.

So the expected quality of the product is one reason why a library or information unit is a logical target for intrapreneuring. Are there others? From the point of view of the information customer, the answer is yes. First of all, information is expensive, and organizations and institutions have invested considerable resources in building up libraries and information services. Much of the information coming out of these services can be of value to other organizations and/or researchers, who may not have the sophisticated resources to obtain information which can be obtained through the library. More important, perhaps, is that the library staff, in their continual quest for better ways to handle the vast quantities of data flowing in and out of the information center, are constantly innovating, constantly seeking new ways to do the work. When these can be shared with others, outside the company, at a profit, the library has taken the first step in paying its own way. For management this can be an exciting and stimulating new concept.

What, then, are some of the specific intrapreneuring ventures that can be attempted in a library or information center? What kinds of information can be sold outside the organization? A simple service which can bring immediate rewards is online literature searching, as indicated earlier. The equipment is in place, the databases are subscribed to, the searcher is available. If these databases can also provide data for others, why shouldn't it be offered and charged at a profit?

From this initial step can come further refinements. A book publisher, for example, has a very small book collection, mostly for the editorial staff. Considerable attention has been given, however, to creating an electronic library. Using the online magazine index created in-house, the publisher – through the editorial library – offers a fee-based information service to the public, answering queries related to its own publications as well as selling photocopies of articles and bibliographies.

Another corporate library in a for-profit environment also went public with fee-based searching and the sale of bibliographies produced in-house, but this library also went public with library consulting, and now provides, for a fee, library consultations to the corporation's clients who need help in solving and analyzing library problems.

Although not in a corporate setting, but certainly motivated by a quest for profit, Marquette University's Memorial Library created an intrapreneurial product in the academic world. The library is the Funding Information Center with a large identified public. For many years, the library has been publishing, for a profit, *Foundations in Wisconsin*, a comprehensive directory of all non-profit organizations in the state of Wisconsin. According to Library Director Kate McCready, the profits from the sale of the directory have provided funds for special purchases for the collection and for travel and conference expenses.

Over ten years ago, the Medical College of Wisconsin, another specialized library, created PRONTO, a comprehensive, rapid biomedical research service. For an annual fee, plus the costs of the searches, PRONTO provides lawyers, healthcare administrators, insurance companies, pharmaceutical and medical suppliers and other professionals with medically related information for their work. Initially, PRONTO grew at a rate of over 16%, but now the growth and the profits have leveled off. PRONTO has become a line item in the library budget. Not only does it provide a valuable service to the staff and the community, it also helps to support library operations.

In addition to providing the data itself, however, highly innovative librarians are often in a position to sell some technology which has been designed for the library. A good case in point is Rya Ben-Shir, Manager of the MacNeal Hospital Health Science Resource Center in Berwyn, Illinois. In 1984, Ben-Shir saw the need for an inexpensive software package for speeding up the interlibrary loan process (and the administrative need for complete usage statistics) for the borrowing library. After a fruitless search the library developed its own software, which it then sold to over 360 sites worldwide; over five years this brought in more than $250,000 in revenue for the hospital. Although the software had two releases, it continually needed updating because of client demands, new releases of DOS, the changing PC environment, and documentation rewrites. Newer releases required $50,000–60,000 in support that ultimately the hospital was unwilling to fund, saying that they were not in the software business. Finally, the software project ceased. Was Ben-Shir bitter or upset? Not at all. She said that the product had been a wonderful springboard both for her and for the hospital. The hospital administrators were very impressed since they didn't expect this result from the library and were not hesitant about giving her additional support. She, too, has personally received benefits from the product, including greater visibility in the library community, networking with librarians around the world, and giving talks on innovation and entrepreneurship. Surprisingly, only $600 was spent on expenses in the first release of the software and yet it brought in $4,000 in the first month. Ben-Shir's entrepreneurial spirit is reflected in her statement, 'Working on the first release with hospital programmers, we undertook this project without the knowledge of the hospital administrators, and we felt like rebels.'

So there are, indeed, intrapreneurial opportunities for information services, and if the corporate environment encourages this kind of innovation, management might consider working with the librarian to explore the opportunities. Where can it lead? Nobody knows. If the organization has a history of solid teamwork, and if the librarian and her managers are willing to take the risks involved, certainly the possibilities are significant. If the intrapreneurial effort is considered merely to pay for the support of the library, motivated by some vague management desire to remove information costs from corporate overheads, the project is doomed to failure. If, on the other hand, the advantages of intrapreneuring are seen to be those of better service for current library users and sharing the resources (which already exist) with others willing to pay for them, the future looks bright indeed.

Perhaps the secret for any success in intrapreneuring in the library comes from the teamwork suggested above. Perhaps it comes from the librarian. More likely, however, it will come from management, who will seek out librarians and information specialists who have the vision, the enthusiasm, the flexibility, and especially the spirit, to see beyond what librarians have always been expected to see. 'Managers must choose intrapreneurs who are persistent, impatient, who laugh, and who face the barriers. Then they have to be willing to trust that the intrapreneurs know how to do their jobs and must give them what they are asking for – resources and people to carry forward their ideas' (Pinchot, 1987, p. 19). Can this happen in a corporate or other specialized library? In other types of information services units? Definitely. And that library or information unit can then show others in the organization that not only are the information services provided for them of the high quality that they demand, but they are so good that others are willing to pay for them.

References

Ben-Shir, Rya. *Interview with Beth Duston*, January, 1995.

Carrier, Camille. 'Intrapreneurship in large firms and SMRs: a comparative study.' *International Small Business Journal*, 12 (3), April–June, 1994.

Davenport, Paul. *Process Innovation: Reengineering Work through Information Technology*. Cambridge MA: Harvard Business School Press, 1993.

Drake, Miriam A. 'Value of the information professional: cost/benefit analysis.' *President's Task Force on the Value of the Information Professional - Final Report, Preliminary Study*. Washington DC: Special Libraries Association, 1987.

Hartman, Curtis. 'Secrets of *Intra*preneuring.' *Inc*, 7 (1), January, 1985.

King, Don and Griffiths, José-Marie. *Special Libraries and Information Services - Increasing the Information Edge*. Rockville MD: Information Frontiers Publications.

Landau, Ralph. 'Corporate partnering can spur innovation.' *Research Management*, May/June, 1987, p.22.

Levitt, Theodore. 'Marketing intangible products and product intangibles.' *Harvard Business Review*, May/June, 1987.

[Macfarlane, Judy.] 'The information interview: Judy Macfarlane at the Price Waterhouse Business Information Center: bringing intrapreneurial services to the Montréal business community'. *InfoManage: The International Management Newsletter for the Information Services Executive*, 2 (8), July, 1995.

Pinchot, Gifford III. 'Innovation through intrapreneuring.' *Research Management*, March/April, 1987.

Pinchot, Gifford III. *Intrapreneuring: Why You Don't Have to Leave the Corporation to Become an Entrepreneur*. New York: Harper & Row, 1985.

Veaner, Allen B. 'Introduction' *President's Task Force on the Value of the Information Professional - Final Report, Preliminary Study*. Washington DC: Special Libraries Association, 1987.

Chapter Twelve

Entrepreneurial rewards

The pleasures of entrepreneurial librarianship are many, and while much of what is attained relates to the success of the organization of which the library is a part, there are also those attainments that characteristically associate with the personal satisfactions that are sought in the workplace. Several of these can be identified. Professional fulfillment, for example, can be an attractive reward as entrepreneurial management moves the information services unit into the enterprise at large and the queries become more and more intellectually challenging and, when successfully negotiated, professionally beneficial. We all work to 'stretch' ourselves, to keep learning new things, to keep moving forward intellectually, and the sense of challenge that the entrepreneurial library offers is frequently a pleasurable experience. Staff stimulation becomes a benefit of employment and it makes the place a better one in which to work.

The entrepreneurial library also brings with it a new and progressive 'culture', a working ambience which is recognized throughout the organization as one which attracts interested, curious users and provides them with a quality of information delivery that goes beyond what is merely required for the transfer of data. It provides an opportunity for staff and users to stay 'fresh' in their interactions with one another, and with the information world at large. Specific benefits can be identified and should be sought by any information services manager who wants his or her unit to be successful.

The workplace: management and staff working together

For many in information services the benefits of entrepreneurial management accrue from the collaborative relationships that develop. In a public library, say, or an academic library, not only does an innovative approach to information delivery result in better relations between the library and its customers, the internal stakeholders, the library's managers, its employees, and its vendors and suppliers all become part of a workforce that Edward Marshall (1995) characterizes as a 'strategic alignment.' It is a linking together of all who have any interest in and any connection whatsoever with the delivery of information from that unit, and it is this collaboration that enables the entrepreneurial manager to integrate the various components of his or her vision.

> In the collaborative workplace, strategic alignment is the process that enables the entire organization to come to a basic agreement on a definition of its unique and value-added role in the marketplace: to identify customer require-ments and to determine the company's competitive advantage and strategies for growth. This means that all the key stakeholders agree to what the orga-nization has decided to do. . . . There are four critical benefits . . .
>
> Building full-scale customer relationships
>
> Assessing the company's unique and value-added role
>
> Identifying the company's market niche
>
> Increasing the stakeholders' sense of ownership
>
> (Marshall, pp. 90–91)

Applying Marshall's collaborative alignment theory in the entrepreneurial information services workplace, it is not difficult to picture how the bene-fits will accumulate. In a private club library, for example, by establishing collaborative relationships between the library and the club members, directors and management, the library manager can build a complete picture of what the information services requirements are and move to provide those services. It permits the library to build that full-scale rela-tionship with its customers that Marshall advocates, and it means that none of the constituent customer base is excluded.

Carrying this illustration further, the library's unique and value-added role in the personal and professional lives of its customers can be assessed, and in those information situations where the library is not meeting needs, steps can be taken to provide services. Conversely, if services are being offered that are not being fully utilized, by having a completely collabo-rative alignment with the various stakeholders in the organization, the library staff can determine which services to reduce or eliminate. Of course having a collaborative alignment with the several types of infor-mation stakeholders enables the library's management to understand exactly what the library's market is, enabling it to concentrate on those activities that result in satisfactory services. Finally, however, and this is probably the most important of Marshall's four benefits, the various stake-holders are brought into the information process and their sense of ownership is increased, thus providing the library with users and people of authority in the organization who have an interest in the success of the information operation. It is this last connection which raises the collaborative alignment to a level of real value to the organization, for – properly executed – a collaborative alignment becomes in effect a lobbying mechanism, an advocacy force for the library, and that makes the library staff's job much easier.

Improved and enhanced information services

One of the primary rewards of entrepreneurial management in information services is the opportunity it affords for the development of new products and services that are wanted and needed. A few years ago, Carol Ginsburg, who manages Bankers Trust Company's international information network, recognized that a new approach to information was coming into play at the bank. She also recognized that this new way of looking at information – she called it 'the information-independent organization' – had come about through a shared interest in information delivery which she, several of the information technology people in the company, and senior management were experiencing. As a result the concept just seemed to fall into place, since they were all trying to manage information. It became an organization-wide policy with the goal of moving toward a more effective delivery of information.

At Bankers Trust the idea was to put as much information as possible in the hands of the individual employees, and both employees and information staff took to the new concept with much enthusiasm. In fact, information workers particularly like the concept because it means that the information center can offer more services and a broader range of resources. So although the workload seemed to increase instead of shrink, there was remarkable staff acceptance. Staff find themselves taking pride in their work and like the fact that their roles are changing, from being traditional providers of information to being information 'navigators' or 'counselors' or 'consultants' for other bank employees.

Users, too, are enthusiastic about the idea of the information-independent organization, because the information provided plays a part in making them successful in their work and so they appreciate its value, especially when it can be provided in a relatively seamless format. Of course some answers still come from books and hard copy resources (about 15% of the information provided, according to Ginsburg), but the primary focus is on online and other automated resources, with as much 'information independence' for the bank's employees as possible.

This move toward a more customer-controlled information interaction is a phenomenon that Joseph J. Fitzsimmons, former President and Chairman of University Microfilms International in Ann Arbor, Michigan, has also identified. He uses the word 'disintermediation' to describe it and characterizes it as a structural change taking place in the information 'chain'.

Such changes are certainly not a problem for the entrepreneurial manager, and any one of them will quickly jump in, as Ginsburg has done, to see that new and better information delivery can be provided. On the other hand, since technology is developing at such a tremendous rate, there is a need to train the information services people who are going to be showing their users how to access this networked information. The non-entrepreneurial information manager sometimes resists because this new 'structural change' frequently does away with the person who mediates between the information and the user. In the past such a person was a gatekeeper or interpreter, and played a very important role in the information transfer process. Now this has changed, and information services workers, authors, aggregators, resellers, distributors, publishers and even the end-users interact all over the place, without mediation. So the entrepreneurial information services manager looks at these changes, determines what his or her staff need to do to replace the mediation role, and moves forth in those new directions. No-one is better trained or philosophically better suited to lead the organization through such changes, and it's a challenge of the highest order, with a payoff that few other management employees can expect.

Matching customer expectations with perceptions

The process begins with changing customer perceptions, because for most lay people the work that goes on in a 'library' or 'information resource center' is usually based on experiences and perceptions that do not match the current situation. At Ashridge Management College in Berkhamstead, England, Andrew Ettinger is the manager of the Learning Resources Centre, a state-of-the-art operation that exists to provide information management and training for the several thousand participants in Ashridge programs. One of Ettinger's major efforts has been to establish that the facility is an 'information and learning center' and not a traditional library, because to the executives and management students who come to Ashridge the 'traditional library' would be off-putting. In fact, Ettinger makes the point that, at the college, they are not shy about moving beyond the traditional orientation in the profession. 'Most managers,' he says, 'do not think very highly of their corporate libraries, and they assume service will be poor. It's our job to change that kind of thinking.'

Change it they do, for with a facility that's open twenty-four hours a day, seven days a week, and staffed for ninety-one hours a week, it is imperative that information staff be able to provide as much as it can in terms of full-service information delivery. Ettinger is obviously attempting to establish another of those 'one-stop shopping' information resources that are becoming more and more prevalent, and so far the results have been good. With so much change taking place in the management field anyway, with flatter organizations, delayering, business process reengineering and more emphasis on flexibility, he insists that the information staff at Ashridge be qualified for many different types of information delivery and help managers learn to utilize a variety of media and technologies.

Ruth Seidman, too, is a proponent of matching customer expectations with perceptions. As head of the Engineering and Science Libraries at Massachusetts Institute of Technology in Cambridge, Massachusetts, Seidman was brought in to facilitate a major reorganization, the administrative merger of the Science Library with the Barker Engineering Library. In the process she came to understand the various demands and requirements of the information stakeholders, and one of the important issues that she and her senior staff looked at carefully was ways in which the delivery of information could reach beyond traditional borders to bring services and products to the users from wherever they are found. It was a natural relationship, for international information issues have long been a major interest of Seidman's. When she was President of the Special Libraries Association in 1990–1991, she had used international information access issues as the theme of her presidency, so she was well qualified to work with MIT faculty and students on this subject.

The Engineering and Science Libraries at MIT have become a vital resource for their information stakeholders in the area of international information, partly due, of course, to the 'amazing effect,' as Seidman characterizes it, of the Internet on information exchange. In almost every subject area in which MIT reference librarians work, they use online sources to access information for the users. And of course it's international. That's what the Internet is all about, and that's what the information stakeholders at MIT want.

The repositioned library

Obviously no entrepreneurially managed information services operation is going to remain static, but the true value of innovative management is reflected in the changes that take place beyond the department. When others in the enterprise begin to perceive its role as different from what it had been in the past, the work of the entrepreneurial manager is successful.

Think about the concept of the 'virtual library,' as it is being deliberated in the business and research community today. Alan Powell has come up with a definition (or variations on a definition). As Powell describes the virtual library, it can be any one of the following:

a library with little or no physical plant of books, periodicals, reading space, or support staff, but one that disseminates selective information directly to distributed library customers, usually electronically.

a more traditional library that has transformed some significant portions of its information delivery channels into electronic format, so that many or most of its customers do not need to visit the library to obtain information.

a library that operates as a nexus of selected information management activities within the organization, some of them centralized, but most of which happen through the efforts of decentralized staff, resources, systems, and even outside suppliers, who are accessible and dispersed throughout the organization. (Powell, p. 260)

'Each of these models,' Powell continues, 'would seem to imply significant changes in management practices. To be sure, they require sophisticated and innovative thinking about both organizations and operations,' and it is that sophisticated and innovative thinking that positions the library or other information services unit in a totally different space in the organizational framework than it ever occupied before.

Both Sylvia Piggott and Patricia Foy have written about what happens when an entrepreneurial librarian achieves success. In Foy's scenario, the users' perceptions of the librarian's role changes, connected with an ongoing effort to reallocate and retrain human resources. Key activities relating to responsibility for information content and vendor contracts are moved to a more centralized framework, and significant progress is made across all lines of business to decide upon the implementation plans necessary for sharing and coordinating resources, enhancing the information infrastructure, eliminating inequalities, establishing an information policy, and networking communications across the entire user population (Foy, p. 52).

For people like Sylvia Piggott, what is happening in information services is revolution, not incremental improvement, and with the entrepreneurial approach 'special librarians and information professionals have a chance to reinvent the library' and bring quality, value-added services to the organizations that employ them. 'Librarians cannot just react to the realities of today's information requirements,' Piggott writes. 'They have to influence them,' to 'take ownership of the information profession.' For Piggott, this means using the techniques of management methodologies such as reengineering and similar processes to improve their services. If they do so,

. . . they will demonstrate their worth to the organization to senior management and will heighten the awareness of senior management of the caliber of the organization's information professionals. This may be one way information professionals can demonstrate their potential to sit in the executive board room alongside other professionals such as lawyers and chartered accountants.

(Piggott, p. 18)

This picture of the information professional as key executive is a very realizable vision, and is based on the application of the same character-istics and qualities that have always characterized executive success: entrepreneurial thinking and innovative management. It has worked for other managers and it can work for librarians.

The greatest reward of all

While this is not a book about what is commonly called 'pop psychology,' we cannot ignore the role of human nature in thinking about the work we do and the satisfactions it brings us. In our professional lives, we crave satisfaction just as we do in our personal lives, and for the lucky ones the satisfactions of the workplace connect with the satisfactions they experience in their personal lives. So it is that almost every entrepreneur/intrapreneur has one scenario, one vision, that outranks almost every other motivation and reward. Some people know it and look forward to the experience. Most, however, have not given them-selves over to intellectualizing the experience that they would like to have, and for them it comes as a wonderful surprise when it happens. What it is, of course, is the pleasure of being able to just sit back and look at what they've done, to bask in the glory of having made a differ-ence, having done something for the organization that no-one else has done. Either no-one else thought of doing this thing, or the support was not there, or the time was not right. But this person came along, saw that an innovative approach to information services could be good for the organization and proceeded to bring that idea to reality. It's an expe-rience unlike any other. No other worker has been able to do what this entrepreneurial librarian has done, and when it happens, whatever trials, whatever frustrations had to be dealt with to get there, suddenly become unimportant. The innovative information services manager has achieved what he or she set out to do, and in today's workplace that is a very nice feeling indeed.

References

Foy, Patricia S. 'The reinvention of the corporate information model – the information professional's role in empowering today's work force.' *The Power of Information: Transforming the World/Professional Papers from the 86th Annual Conference of the Special Libraries Association, June 10-15, 1995, Montréal, Quebec, Canada.* Washington, DC: Special Libraries Association, 1995.

Marshall, Edward M. *Transforming the Work We Do: the Power of the Collaborative Workplace*. New York: American Management Association, 1995.

Piggott, Sylvia. 'Why corporate librarians must reengineer the library for the new information age.' *Special Libraries*, 86 (1), Winter, 1995.

Powell, Alan. 'Management models and measurement in the virtual library.' *Special Libraries*, 85 (4), Fall, 1994.

Chapter thirteen
Can we do it?

By now, it should be very clear to the reader that this book is very much influenced by my own perceptions and understandings of the library and information services field. I am very aware that many people - both within the profession and outside it - do not have the same perceptions as I have about the work we do. Still, I can't help but wonder if there isn't some focal point that will bring us closer together in our various points of view. If so, it seems appropriate to give some thought to the future of information services, and particularly the future of librarianship. Let me describe some of my ideas about where I think the profession is going.

This approach is not quite as prideful as it seems, for I am a continual observer of the profession. Not only am I a librarian by training, the company which employs me is a consulting and training firm, and for both of these activities we are required to be aware of what's happening in the profession. We also are responsible, as a publishing company, for delivering to our subscribers two newsletters, *The One-Person Library: A Newsletter for Librarians and Management*, for the librarian who works alone, and *InfoManage: The International Management Newsletter for the Information Services Executive*, for those who have management responsibility for information services for their organizations. Keeping up with librarianship and information services is what we do.

A first observation must rightly be that this is an exciting time for library and information services professionals. Our ability to access and manipulate information with speed, accuracy and sophistication makes us vital players in the much-heralded 'information age.' At the same time, our ability and our willingness to continue to offer what many of us in the profession refer to as 'traditional' library services defines us as one of society's few truly service professions, for librarians, unlike many others who play a 'service' role in society, have continued to offer their services, in one form or another, regardless of the difficulties and undaunted by the failures. Of difficulties and failures there have been, of course, any number; yet, despite them and despite the setbacks, we librarians are a hearty lot. We can always be counted on to come through.

But things might change. Now, as we approach the twenty-first century, a new cry is being heard. Now librarians are beginning to ask if they should, in fact, be providing those services, especially if they are not appreciated and not properly funded. We are beginning to wonder if we should be offering our services whether or not they are valued and whether or not they are supported. We are beginning to wonder if we should, in fact, be the lone, lorn altruists of society, for until now it seems this was to be our destiny.

Perhaps not. Some have taken it upon themselves to try to challenge the profession about some of these issues. In 1991, for example, after I made my inaugural speech as president of the Special Libraries Association, after I had challenged the profession to take a long, hard look at who we are bringing into special librarianship for the next century, I was lambasted by my critics for daring to say aloud that some of our people aren't good enough to do the work we're supposed to be doing. My message was one no-one wanted to hear. But some of our people really are not good enough to be special librarians. I was proposing that we look at how we recruit people into this branch of the profession, and this fact must be acknowledged if we are going to recruit the best. To those who agreed with me, I was simply telling it like it is and simply asking questions that had not been asked before.

Much the same thing happened in San Francisco, when I ended my presidency and called on our very fine association, which has the potential to be the leading information services association in the world, to embrace that leadership potential by changing what we call ourselves and by organizing a serious, directed effort to bring the best people in. After two years of saying these things to anyone who would listen, including the members of some 36 chapters all around the world, I did not think that what I had said in San Francisco had been particularly radical. By this time, I figured that my ideas about special librarianship were 'old hat' for most of the members of the SLA. Not so, for after the speech one of the most important library leaders in America, a person who probably has more influence than anyone else in librarianship today, came up to me and said, 'Interesting speech, Guy – but you don't believe all that stuff, do you?'

Believe it? How could I not believe it? I had just said it to a thousand people. And yet this person, this leader, could not take me seriously.

So what are we talking about, when we speak of 'the future of librarianship'? I think what we are dealing with is change, and with change management, and the future of librarianship is going to depend, in great part on how we as librarians adapt to the changes that society, technology, and our own profession will have forced upon us in the next few years. In fact, the future of librarianship looks very exciting and promising, if we will accept three basic facts about libraries and information, and the role that librarians are going to be able to play in the future.

First of all, service to the customer will continue to be required. The people for whom we provide library and information services, and it does not matter whether we call them 'patrons', 'users', 'readers', or whatever else we have called them for the past hundred years or so, expect the same level of service satisfaction they receive in their other interactions. The message I get from users all the time is that in their dealings with librarians they expect to be treated as 'customers,' so I happen to prefer that term. But it really doesn't matter what we call them. What does matter is that they are satisfied with the services and products we provide for them, and if we want them to continue to come to us, we must not only provide them with what they need, we must also provide value-added services as well, just as any other business does.

But what kind of service are we providing today, and how concerned are we that our customers be satisfied? In many cases libraries have become so institutionalized and bureaucratized, and the interests of our customers have become so distanced from the institutions that serve them, that it is a wonder anyone comes to us. Do I exaggerate? Michael Gorman wrote a very important article many years ago. I quote it frequently, for to my way of thinking this is the only way to define what we do. A library, Gorman said, is 'library service from the library user's point of view' because, 'to any library user, the question is not a building, or a collection, or an administrative structure.' It is, 'are the materials and services available to me when I need them?' (Gorman, p. 325).

Is this the kind of library we manage? Does this define the service we offer to our users? Of course not, for our libraries have become top-heavy with rules, regulations, restrictions and restraints, all in the name of the institution, the library itself. All this is not important to the library user or to the prospective library user; all he or she wants are the materials and services, when he or she needs them. Everything else gets in the way. In this day and age users, demanding quick responses in everything else they do – shopping, banking, instant replays on the television and so on – demand the same of us. And we delude ourselves if we think we can ask them to wait: we can't and they won't, they'll go somewhere else and get those materials and services when and as fast as they need them.

This shouldn't be a problem for us, and the fact that it is creates much of the tension we experience within the profession. Why is it that our institutions become so important in themselves that they take over and prevent us delivering what our customers want? We understand service and the proper application of customer service techniques in the work we do. We know that our job is to get the information to the user. Whatever form this information takes, we librarians know how to deliver it: it's what we've been trained to do but we don't do it. Excellence in the provision of information products and services is what will carry us successfully into the future. What prevents us from providing excellence in customer service? We had better find out, or there won't be any libraries for us to be delivering services from in the not-too-distant future. We must find out why there is this dichotomy in our profession, this tension between knowing how to deliver excellence in customer service and not doing it.

A second fact that will affect our future success has to do with the organization of information. And the role we are given to play in that work. Now I don't need to write here about the volume of information, about how much of it there is, about how we're all drowning in a sea of 'data' and because there is so much of it, no one can pull out the 'knowledge'. All of this has been written about many times by people who are much better versed in the subject and certainly more articulate that I am, but I think there are some points we might consider. We should be leading the way in this area, and if we're not, why aren't we? No-one

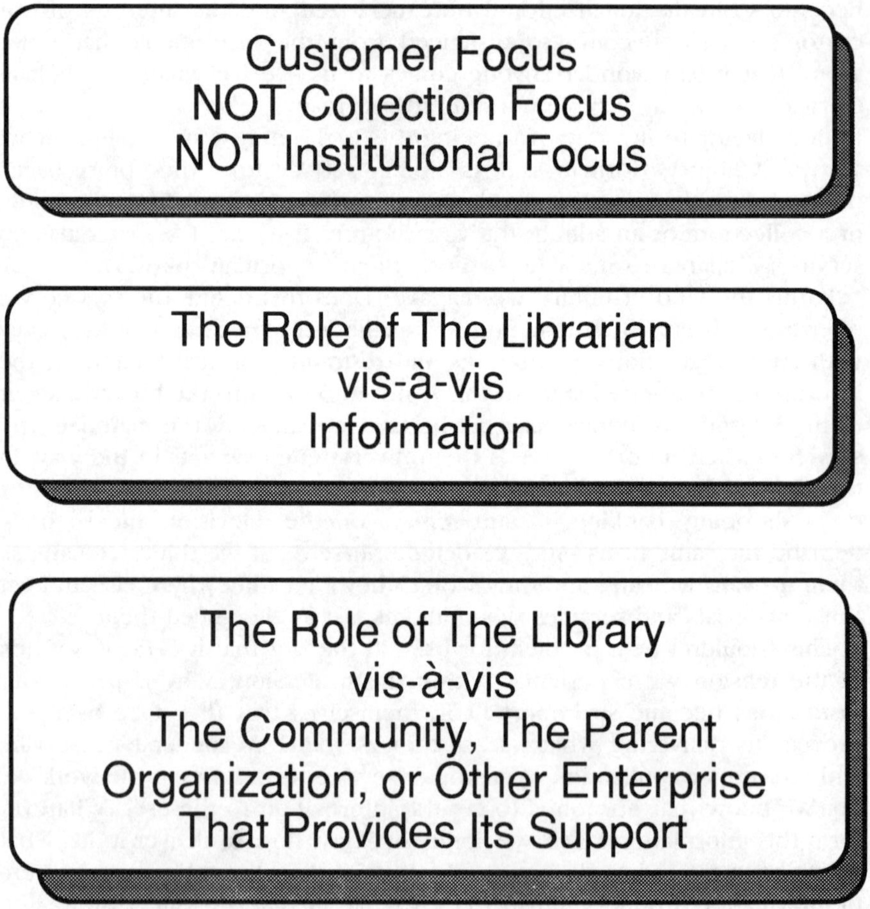

Customer Focus
NOT Collection Focus
NOT Institutional Focus

The Role of The Librarian
vis-à-vis
Information

The Role of The Library
vis-à-vis
The Community, The Parent
Organization, or Other Enterprise
That Provides Its Support

Figure 13.1   Librarianship: a survival kit for the 21st century

understands it better than we do. Within the organizations where we work there are other people involved in information services. Do any of them – corporate archivist, chief of records management, even MIS staff – know as much about the organization of information as a librarian does? Does anyone else have the librarian's experience, skills, background and authority in the organization and management of information? Of course not, yet few librarians become CIOs in their companies, few are involved in determining information policy, and certainly few librarians are called upon for advice when the company is considering downsizing or otherwise reorganizing its information operations.

Why not? What is it about our profession that prevents the decision makers from seeking our advice? For example, one of the most exciting concepts in our profession today has to do with the integration of all information within an organization: when an integrated information system is in place, the entire organization benefits. Yet where does the idea come from? It was special librarians such as Elizabeth Orna, Betty Eddison, Ken Megill, Sarah Kadek and others who came up with the concept. Yet when librarians go to managers with the idea they are surprised that it came from us. Managers don't expect librarians to understand the organization of information, yet no-one understands it better. The organization of information will be critical to the future success of any community or organization and librarians can play a very important part if we will put ourselves forward. Will we?

A third fact that must be recognized is the changing role of the library. What are we supposed to be? Are we doing ourselves and our customers a disservice by trying to be all the things that a 'library' is expected to be? Are we failing our customers, our managers and the organizations which employ us, by trying to do too much? Vivienne Monty wrote an article in which she made reference to some libraries that offered as many as two hundred different services to their users (Monty, pp. 1–5), despite cutbacks in funding, downsizing, and similar restrictive activities. My question is: were any of these services any good?

It seems to me that librarians have a responsibility to avoid trying to be all things to all people, and that's very hard when the age-old concept of 'library' means that anything anyone asks for will be available. As we go into the future we must look at what our mission is supposed to be, change it if it is no longer appropriate, and work with our managers and our customers to determine just which services we should be offering. While this might appear to contradict what I wrote earlier about serving the customers, providing for their needs, it does not for in fact to be able to provide for any customers at the highest level of service quality, we must pick and choose what we do. We can't do it all (and in fact, we never could, but we pretended for many decades that we could), so we must cut back so that the things we do offer can be the things we do well.

This means that the continuing tension between 'traditional' library services and 'information management' will probably escalate into a division – which from my point of view is healthy for us all. Libraries and librarianship are but one part of the overall information services 'umbrella'. This is a construct that embraces not only librarianship, but such other fields as archives, records management, information brokering, consulting, publishing and even, to a certain extent, MIS, communications and telecommunications and a whole host of others who are involved with the organization, management and distribution of information. (Figure 13.1).

What is happening, it seems to me, is that the lines of demarcation between the various groups that make up 'information services' are becoming more and more pronounced, and new alliances are being forged, 'strategic alliances' that are going to result in better service to more specifically defined customers. Take special librarianship, for example: what has happened in the last few years? Specialized librarians find that many of their ideas about the provision of information services and products not only don't match those of traditional librarianship in general, in some cases they actually conflict. A case in point concerns training. The decision makers in many organizations seeking to hire someone to offer information services – a 'special librarian' – couldn't care less about the library profession's educational criteria, and frequently employ a person who does not have a master's degree in library and information studies. And what happens? That person goes to work in that organization, learns what is needed, learns how to provide it, and becomes an excellent special librarian without ever having set foot in a graduate library program. Such a scenario tells us much about how specialized librarianship and librarianship in general, despite much that is shared, have drifted in different directions in response to the specific needs of their users.

And there is another, more portentous scenario looming on the horizon, for in May 1995 the leaders of the library and information services community in Germany met to discuss a new role for one-person librarians.The event, in Berlin, was called The First German One-Person Library Round Table, and it is very likely that similar meetings will be held in other places in the near future. It was organized by Evelin Morgenstern of the Deutsches Bibliotheksinstitut, who pointed out that 'one-person librarianship is a subject that has to be discussed in its own right. It is not a reduced or shrunken version of something else. It is in and of itself a viable part of the information services profession.' With so many organizations seeking a single employee to be in charge of information delivery, and with internal and external information being more and more integrated under the responsibility of that one employee, leaders in organizational management, and in the information services field, are beginning to question whether training for librarianship is appropriate for these people. In fact, it is now recognized that one-person librarianship is a distinct discipline within information services. One-person librarians are respected for their success in what they do, and their work is not seen as an 'abbreviated' or 'less-than-whole' version of some other construct of library or information work. Do we dare predict that at some future data one-person information specialists will not be part of the library profession at all? It could happen ('OPLs in Germany . . .' pp. 1–5).

As far as the future of librarianship is concerned, these sorts of divisions will be exacerbated. We will see more such divisions, and it might not be such a bad thing for I'm not sure that the concerns of a children's librarian in a rural community are particularly relevant to the work done by the manager of information services for a major financial institution, or vice versa. The division between those who provide public library service (with its specific philosophy of librarianship as social work) and those who are employed in the more specialized library community couldn't be greater, and it is nowhere more earnestly manifested than in many of the students who come into librarianship. When they are confronted with management courses, as opposed to courses in how a library is used to provide educational and social services for the community, and when attempts are made to bring a management perspective to the 'administration' of libraries, many of them are visibly upset, for they see the study of management as undermining the philosophy of librarianship that they have been exposed to and accept. They are quite open in their allegiance to the social role of libraries, to the educational work that they expect to do as librarians. Of course we wish them well, but why are they not studying in the graduate education department or the graduate school of social work. Why then have they come to a graduate program in library and information services?

These then are the three considerations that I have identified as affecting our work as librarians in the future. We will be required to excel in the application of quality customer service techniques to deliver information services and products; we will be required to participate in the organization of information: and, as traditional librarianship and information delivery become more and more disparate, we will separate into those subgroups of librarianship that best serve the needs of their identified constituent customers. We will no longer be able to be all things to all people.

Can we be successful as librarians in the future? Of course. But we must be prepared to manage our libraries with these three facts in mind. It will not be easy, and it will be made more difficult depending on how we plan for the future, for there are three barriers which must first be overcome before we can be successful as librarians in the future. Unless steps are taken, and taken soon, to overcome these barriers, we don't have a ghost of a chance of succeeding in the future and we will, in fact, be replaced by other, more aggressive sectors of the information services field. The barriers to our success are these: our professional arrogance, the quality of librarianship recruits, and the perceptions others have of us.

Why do I begin with a reference to professional arrogance? Because, alas, I can think of no other term to adequately describe what a non-librarian feels when he or she approaches the reference desk in a library or information center. There is something about our profession that carries an aura of not only knowing the answer before the customer has even asked the question, but which assumes as well a judgmental or evaluative posture that is positively intimidating. Information and the information products that we control are important, but in this day and age (as a reading of any of Tom Peters' books will tell you), the successful organization is the one in which information is open and available, and in which every effort is made to get as much information to as many people as possible, a total reversal of the kind of information management many librarians provide. Of course some

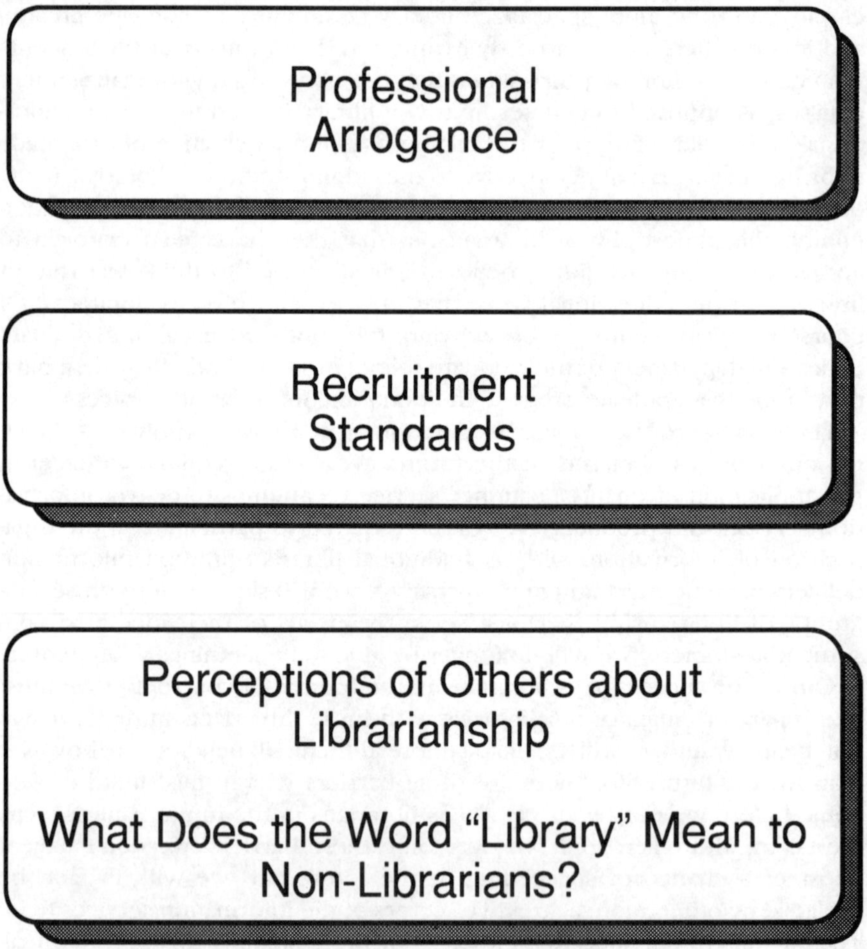

Professional Arrogance

Recruitment Standards

Perceptions of Others about Librarianship

What Does the Word "Library" Mean to Non-Librarians?

Figure 13.2   Librarianship: barriers to survival as we enter the 21st century

have been able to rise above such attitudes, and one business librarian, known to many in her professional community, will not permit such posturing. In fact, she spends a great deal of time ensuring that her staff understand that they are 'just another department,' in the organization. She has no use for those librarians who see themselves as moral arbiters and gatekeepers, whose job it is to decide who gets what information. That kind of arrogance doesn't sit too well in her organization.

But there is other professional arrogance that gets in the way of our success. The man who spoke to me after my speech in San Francisco, for example, was arrogant in his assumption that the things I had to say were not appropriate for that forum. Whether they were right or wrong, or deserved to be said, was irrelevant: a special librarian was saying things about librarianship in general that – in that man's opinion – weren't supposed to be said, and he couldn't resist letting me know.

That same arrogance also occasionally takes on a different tone that does the profession equal harm, for many people who have gone into librarianship don't often like themselves very much, and a destructive attitude comes into play which might be called 'the arrogance of humility.' There are many times when our services are taken for granted, or ignored altogether, and our role in society often falls pretty far down the list when it comes to determining which services our society really needs, but we are often the cause of our own distress. I was dismayed not too long ago when, in a seminar I was leading, one of the attendees took me to task for suggesting – in a case study we used – that the single-staff public librarian for a small community should have been more assertive in seeking a higher wage from the authorities. This person indicated that she worked for her community for less than the minimum wage, and she was proud to do it for, as she said, 'my husband and I have raised and educated our children in the community, we've gained much from the community, and I feel it's appropriate to give something back.'

When another member of the group asked her if, as a professional librarian, she shouldn't receive at least as much as the county employees who provide garbage and police service, she was quick to reply: 'Oh, no,' she said. 'Those are *essential* services.' And *she* emphasized the word 'essential.'

So if we are to succeed as librarians and information managers, perhaps we need to soften up a little about ourselves, about our work, and about the people we serve. Our professional arrogance prevents us from being one of the 'kinder, gentler' professions, which is too bad, for the people who come to us really do respect and admire us for what we can do for them, until we turn them off with our own self-importance (Figure 13.2).

The second barrier concerns recruitment into the profession, and we simply must devise methods for finding the best, brightest and most qualified people to join us. We must begin early, for it has been demonstrated that even people entering graduate schools of library and information studies often have no clear understanding of what librarianship is about, and certainly they don't know what the more specialized librarians do. Every effort must be made, on all levels, to ensure that people contemplating career decisions know about and are drawn to librarianship.

On this subject, it seems to me that the time has come to recognize that the future of librarianship and information services belongs to the young. We must now enter into strong mentoring relationships, to encourage idealistic, innovative, risk-taking young people to enter our profession. We must encourage them to look at library and information services as a dynamic, valuable part of the social fabric, and we must do everything we can to compensate them, to encourage them and to stretch them.

Can we do it? Can young people with enthusiasm be enticed into the library and information services profession? It would be a shame to think that by the time they are ready to select their careers, they may not consider librarianship an option. If we are to maintain and improve our profession, we must give careful thought to why so many talented and gifted young people will seek careers in other fields. What is it about librarianship that turns them off?

We must also give some attention to how recruits are being prepared for the profession, whether they are getting the best preparation. One of our colleagues has pointed out that the only recommendation from the White House Conference on Library and Information Services that addressed the subject of graduate education had as its basis a call for more 'convenient' (his term) education – that is, the location of more graduate library schools nearer applicants' homes. There was no concern about the quality of the education and yet it is this that our critics are shouting about. Do we actually need more graduate library schools? Or do we instead need perhaps a system of triage for those institutions currently offering graduate training, so that the quality of the education, not the location of the school, is our primary focus?

Similarly, shouldn't we recognize that many information services employees are – and will continue to be – engaged by decision makers who do not have our understanding and our requirements for a graduate employee, or any interest in our requirements? If we recognize this fact, we will provide training not graduate education. And we will make it the best it can be, so that employees without graduate education can do their best work while we, the library managers with the graduate degrees, do our best work.

Perhaps what I'm suggesting here is one of those paradigm shifts we hear so much about. One popular lecturer on the subject talks about the different kinds of paradigm people, and we might think about this as we look at who is coming into our profession. This speaker notes that there are the Paradigm Pioneers (usually, he says, the guys with the arrows in their backs) the leaders and managers who encourage revolutionary thinking, who like having mavericks around. On the other hand, there are also the Paradigm Settlers, those who are very pleased that the Pioneers went in and did the work and who are happy to settle in with the status quo.

So we must ask of practitioners: who are you mentoring into librarianship? Who are you encouraging to become librarians and information services professionals? Are you bringing in the Pioneers? The Settlers? Or are you bringing in the people who stayed back east? It's something we have to think about if we're going to make it to the twenty-first century.

Finally, we must change the perceptions lay people have about libraries and librarianship. I do not say that we should change our image: this comes from the quality of the work we do, and if we concentrate on providing quality service we don't have to worry about image. But we can do something about the public's perception about libraries and librarianship and we must. Here is a text that is worth reading:

> Again, lest we become confused and forgetful, the function of a great library is to store obscure books. This is above all the task we want libraries to perform: to hold on to books that we don't want enough to own, books of very limited appeal. . . . A book whose presence you crave at your bedside or whose referential or snob value you think you will need throughout life, you buy. Libraries are repositories for the out of print and the less desired, and we value them inestimably for that. The fact that most library books seldom circulate is part of the mystery and power of libraries. The books are there, waiting from age to age until their moment comes. And in the case of any given book, its moment may never come – but we have no way of predicting that, since we are unable to know now what a future time will find of interest. (Baker, p.37)

Many readers will of course recognize this passage from the famous *New Yorker* article about libraries disposing of their card catalogs. It's quoted here not because this might be a discussion of the pros and cons of automated catalogs but to impress upon readers the public perception of what libraries are. And of course librarians are perceived in the same way. To be fair, Baker represents only one part of the public, but what a part it is! He represents the scholarly community, and look at what he thinks of libraries and librarianship! Is it any wonder that when you tell someone you're a librarian they look at you in disbelief?

So my strongest recommendation for us as librarians is to get rid of the term 'library'. We don't work in what people generally think of as a 'library,' yet we call ourselves librarians. We are, I've heard it said, the only profession that calls itself after the place where the profession is practiced, and for many that name is a problem. Doctors aren't called 'hospitalarians', lawyers aren't called ' courthousians', teachers aren't called 'schoolarians' or 'universitarians' or 'collegians' and preachers and priests aren't called 'chucharians', so why should we be called 'librarians'? We don't hoard obscure books but that's what people think librarians do, and as long as we call ourselves 'librarians' – in this information age, for heaven's sake, in the age of the Internet! – we have already created a barrier that prevents us from serving the customer as well as we can. Obviously I don't know what we will call ourselves, and in the end, probably a great many descriptors will be used, because we all do so many different things that one word probably can't describe us all, but I do know this: the word librarian doesn't do it and, worse, it harms us. We must move away from the term.

So these are my personal ideas about the future of the profession, the three facts of our professional work that must be addressed, and the three barriers to our success. The time has come, it seems to me, to begin to think about these issues together, and we must, because if we don't we won't have a profession to worry about.

This is a radical statement, so let me tell you what I mean. In our society today, information is acknowledged as necessary for just about everything we do. Particularly in the business community, in diplomacy, in science information makes things happen. Yet those who recognize the value of information typically go to sources other than libraries for that information, and this is of concern to me. It seems that other segments of society are handling much of the information the decision makers need, and while these other information providers have become stronger and stronger, librarianship, for a variety of reasons, has not kept up. We've fallen considerably behind, and we need to work very hard to re-establish our authoritative, our essential, role in society.

In writing about our future I have perhaps raised some tough questions that we as practitioners must ask. Moving into a consideration of entrepreneurial management for the library and information services field, there should be some prospects for a less bleak and even bright future. Of course we must take a hard, long look at what is wrong with our profession, but in doing so perhaps we'll shift our paradigms, so that past models of librarianship will be re-examined in light of what we need to do, not just today, but as we go into this new era that I, and others, are referring to as a 'golden age of information services'. I hope we'll scan the environment in which we operate so that we can plan strategically, accepting that change is both inevitable and desirable, an idea which has, until now, threatened us and frightened us.

Librarianship has much potential as a profession, and librarians can do much for society and themselves with the contributions they make. But we must take the initiative ourselves for if we do not we will regret it. To illustrate, we can think about an image a colleague has come up with. This person, also a consultant, works on many library/information services projects and thus has plenty of opportunity to observe the differences between what we as professionals think about libraries and what those outside the profession think about our work.

My colleague tells it like this: as far as library and information services are concerned, the train is in the station, and it's ready to leave. Now we have the opportunity to get on that train and move into the 21st century, into that much-heralded information age. But we have to make the decision to get on the train. Unfortunately, many of our colleagues won't make this decision. They're satisfied to wait around until their train comes in, – the train that will take them comfortably into some library-land, some fantasy they have of what librarianship should be. But what they don't know, or won't admit, is that that train doesn't stop here any more. It's not even running any more, and if they keep waiting, the train that's sitting here—which is going to leave the station very soon, (in fact, we had better look fast, for it might already have left), that train is the one to be on, and if we're not on it, we won't be able to claim our role in the information services profession of the future. Let's not get left behind.

References

Baker, Nicholson. 'Annals of scholarship: discards.' *New Yorker*, April 4, 1994.

Drucker, Peter F. *Innovation and Entrepreneurship: Practice and Principles*. New York: Harper & Row, 1985.

Gorman, Michael. 'Laying siege to the fortress library: a vibrant technological web connecting resources and users will spell its end.' *American Libraries*, 17 (5), 1986.

Monty, Vivienne. 'Why don't you get your priorities straight?' *The SpeciaList* (Washington DC: Special Libraries Association), 16 (6), June, 1993.

'OPLs in Germany move to enhance status; formal steps taken to structure one-person librarianship as 'a distinct discipline' in information services. *The One-Person Library: A Newsletter for Librarians and Management*, 12 (2), June, 1995.

Selected bibliography

Abram, Stephen. 'Sydney Claire, SLA Professional Award Winner 2005: Transformational Librarianship in Action.' *Special Libraries*, 84 (4), Fall, 1993.

Albrecht, Karl. *The Northbound Train*. New York: American Management Association, 1994.

Baker, Nicholson. 'Annals of scholarship: discards.' *New Yorker*, April 4, 1994.

Balachandran, Sarojini. 'Entrepreneurship in libraries.' *Library Administration and Management*, Spring, 1989.

Barker, Joel. *Paradigms: The Business of Discovering the Future*, New York: HarperBusiness, 1993.

Barrier, Michael. 'Small firms put quality first.' *Nation's Business*, 80 (5), May, 1992.

Begley, Thomas M. and David P. Boyd. 'A comparison of entrepreneurs and managers of small business firms.' *Journal of Management*, 13 (1), 1987.

Bender, David R., Sarah T. Kadec, and Sandy I. Morton, *National Information Policies: Strategies for the Future*. Washington DC: Special Libraries Association, 1991.

Bennett, Lettie. 'The real story behind the new 'library-less campus.' *InfoManage: The International Management Newsletter for the Information Services Executive*, 2(6), May, 1995.

Bennis, Warren, and Burt Nanus. *Leaders: The Strategies for Taking Charge*. New York: Harper and Row, 1985.

Bennis, Warren. *On Becoming a Leader*. New York: Addison-Wesley, 1989.

Bennis, Warren. *Why Leaders Can't Lead*. San Francisco, CA: Jossey-Bass, 1990.

Besant, L. X. 'Transformational librarians and entrepreneurial librarians: are they different?' *Special Libraries*, 84 (4), Fall, 1993.

Birley, Sue. 'The role of networks in the entrepreneurial process.' *Journal of Business Venturing*, 1, Winter, 1986.

Block, Peter. *Stewardship: Choosing Service Over Self-Interest*, San Francisco, CA: Berrett-Koehler, 1993.

Brandt, S. C. *Entrepreneuring: the Ten Commandments for Building a Growth Company*. New York: New American Library, 1988.

Cargill, Jennifer. 'Creativity and innovation in public service.' *Journal of Library Administration*, 10 (2/3), 1989.

Carland, James W., Jo Ann C. Carland, Frank Hoy and William R. Boulton. 'Distinctions between entrepreneurial and small business ventures.' *International Journal of Management*, 6 (1), March, 1988.

Carrier, Camille. 'Intrapreneurship in large firms and SMRs: a comparative study.' *International Small Business Journal*, 12 (3), April–June, 1994.

Champion, Brian. 'Intrapreneuring and the Spirit of Innovation in Libraries.' *Journal of Library Administration*, 9 (2), 1988.

Chell, E. and J.M. Haworth. 'Entrepreneurship and entrepreneurial management: the need for a paradigm.' *Graduate Management Research*, 4, Winter, 1988.

Cluff, E. Dale. 'Developing the entrepreneurial spirit: the director's role.' *Journal of Library Administration*, 10 (2/3), 1989.

Coffman, Steve and Helen Josephine. 'Doing it for money.' *Library Journal*, October, 15, 1991.

Cohen, William A. *The Art of the Leader*. Englewood Cliffs, NJ: Prentice-Hall, 1990.

Cook, James R. *The Start-Up Entrepreneur*. New York: E.P. Dutton, 1985.

Cottam, Keith M. 'Professional identity and 'intrapreneurial' behavior.' *Journal of Library Administration*, 8 (1), Spring, 1987.

Cunningham, J.B. and J. Lischeron. 'Defining entrepreneurship.' *Journal of Small Business Management*, 29 (1), January, 1991.

Davenport, Paul. *Process Innovation: Reengineering Work Through Information Technology*. Cambridge, MA: Harvard Business School Press, 1993.

Davidow, William H. and Michael S. Malone. 'Rethinking management.' *The Virtual Corporation*, New York: HarperCollins, 1992.

Davis, Stan and Bill Davidson. *2020 Vision: Transform Your Business Today to Succeed in Tomorrow's Economy*. New York: Simon and Schuster, 1992.

Deeks, J. *The Small Firm Owner/Manager: Entrepreneurial Behavior and Management Practice*. New York: Praeger, 1976.

'Defining the corporate library: Richard A. Willner at Lehman Brothers.' *InfoManage: The International Management Newsletter for the Information Services Executive*, 1 (8), July, 1994.

Doherty, Walter E. 'Toward the law library as a profit center.' *Journal of Library Administration*, 7 (1), Spring, 1986.

Downes, Robin N. 'Managing for Innovation in the Age of Information Technology.' *Journal of Library Administration*, 8 (1), Spring, 1987.

Drabenstott, Karen M. *Analytical Review of the Library of the Future*. Washington DC: Council on Library Resources, 1994.

[Drake, Miriam A.] Mimi Drake at Georgia Tech: Ten Years Online and The Future is NOW!' *InfoManage: The International Management Newsletter for the Information Services Executive*, 2 (6), May, 1995.

Drake, Miriam A. 'Policy: help or hurdle?' in *Fee-Based Services: Issues and Answers - Proceedings of The Second Conference on Fee-Based Research in College and Research Libraries*, University of Michigan, May 10-12, 1987, Ann Arbor, MI: Michigan Information Transfer Source, University of Michigan Libraries, 1987.

Drake, Miriam A, 'Value of the information professional: cost/benefit analysis,' *President's Task Force on the Value of the Information Professional - Final Report, Preliminary Study*. Washington, DC: Special Libraries Association, 1987.

Drucker, Peter F. *Innovation and Entrepreneurship: Practice and Principles*. New York: Harper & Row, 1985.

Drucker, Peter F. *Managing for the Future: the 1990s and Beyond*. New York: Truman Talley Books, 1992.

Drucker, Peter F. *Managing the Nonprofit Organization: Principles and Practices*. New York: HarperCollins, 1990.

Drucker, Peter F. 'Tomorrow's restless managers' *Industry Week*, April 18, 1988,

Dumont, Paul E. 'Creativity, innovation, and entrepreneurship in technical services.' *Journal of Library Administration*, 10 (2/3), 1989.

Duston, Beth. 'Getting to the right answer,' in Matarazzo, James M., and Miriam A. Drake. *Information for Management: A Handbook*. Washington DC: Special Libraries Association, 1994.

Duston, Beth. 'How to pick an information broker.' *Library Management Quarterly*, 13, Winter, 1990.

Duston, Beth. 'Managing an information company.' Presentation to The New England Online Users Group, Westborough, MA, November, 1987.

Duston, Beth. 'Marketing within the corporate structure.' Contributed Paper, Special Libraries Association 77th Annual Conference, Boston, MA, 1986.

Duston, Beth. 'On being an entrepreneur.' Presentation to the American Chemical Society, Boston Chapter, Waltham, MA, October, 1988.

Duston, Beth. 'The real cost of information.' *Corptech Focus*, 3, Summer, 1991.

Duston, Beth. 'The fugitive user.' *The One-Person Library: A Newsletter for Librarians and Management*, 10 (2), June, 1993.

Duston, Beth, and Guy St. Clair. 'Mining the company library.' *Growth Strategies/ American Management Association*, November, 1987.

The Entrepreneur's Guide. New York: Research Institute of America, 1986.

Euster, Joanne R. 'Creativity and leadership.' *Journal of Library Administration*, 10 (2/3), 1989.

Ferguson, Elizabeth and Emily R. Mobley. *Special Libraries at Work*, Hamden, CT: The Shoe String Press, 1984.

Ferriero, David S. and T.L. Wilding. 'Scanning the Environment in Strategic Planning.' *Masterminding Tomorrow's Information - Creative Strategies for the '90s*, Washington DC: Special Libraries Association, 1991.

Fineman, H. 'The 'info' entrepreneurs.' *Newsweek*, November 11, 1985.

Foy, Patricia S. 'The re-invention of the corporate information model - the information professional's role in empowering today's workforce.' *The Power of Information: Transforming the World/Professional Papers from the 86th Annual Conference of the Special Libraries Association, June 10-15, 1995, Montréal, Quebec, Canada*. Washington DC: Special Libraries Association, 1995.

Gardner, John W. *Self-Renewal: The Individual and the Innovative Society*. New York: Harper Colophon, 1965.

Gardner, John W. *The Nature of Leadership - The Tasks of Leadership - The Heart of the Matter (Leader-Constituent Interaction.)* Washington DC: Independent Sector, 1986.

Garfield, Charles. 'The innovation imperative.' *Second to None: How Our Smartest Companies Put People First*. Homewood, IL: Business One Irwin, 1992.

Geneen, H. 'Why intrapreneurship doesn't work.' *Venture*, 7 (1), 1985.

Gertzog, Alice, ed. *Leadership in the Library/Information Profession; Proceedings of the 26th Annual Symposium of the Graduate Alumni and Faculty of The Rutgers School of Communication, Information and Library Studies, 8 April 1988.* Jefferson, NC: McFarland, 1989.

Ginsberg, Ari, and Michael Hay. 'Confronting the challenges of corporate entrepreneurship: guidelines for venture managers.' *European Management Journal*, 12 (4), December, 1994.

Gorman, Michael. 'Laying siege to the fortress library: a vibrant technological web connecting resources and users will spell its end.' *American Libraries*, 17 (5), 1986.

Hafner, Katie. 'Wiring the ivory tower.' *Newsweek*, January 30, 1995.

Hagner, Thomas H. 'How to cultivate company culture.' *Personal Selling Power*, November/December, 1994.

Hammer, Michael and James Champy. *Reengineering the Corporation: A Manifesto for Business Revolution*. New York: HarperCollins, 1993.

Hammer, Michael and Steven A. Stanton. *The Reengineering Revolution*. New York: HarperCollins, 1995.

Hartman, Curtis. 'Secrets of *Intra*preneuring.' *Inc*, 7 (1), January, 1985.

Hayes, Robert M. *Strategic Management for Academic Libraries*. Westport, CT: Greenwood Press, 1993.

'Hierarchy? Flat? Or *Web*? What's your management style?' *InfoManage: The International Management Newsletter for the Information Services Executive*, 2 (7), June, 1995.

Hinshaw, Marilyn L. 'Strategies used in developing library support.' *Journal of Library Administration*, 10 (2/3), 1989.

Hisrich, R.D. 'Entrepreneurship/intrapreneurship.' *American Psychologist*, 45, 1990.

Hogeveen, H. and R. Jones. 'Paradox, paragon, or paralysis? Three organizations in 2005.' *Special Libraries*, 84 (4), Fall, 1993.

Horton, Forest Woody Jr. *Extending the Librarian's Domain: A Survey of Emerging Occupation Opportunities for Librarians and Information Professionals*. Washington DC: Special Libraries Association, 1994.

Huffman, F. 'Information for sale: brokers provide answers to an information-hungry America for unquestionable profits.' *Entrepreneur*, January, 1988.

Hughes, Carol. 'Librarians as innovators.' *Journal of Library Administration*, 10 (2/3), 1989.

'Information brokers: who, what, why, how.' *Bulletin of the American Society for Information Science*, 2 (7), 1976.

'Information, please: entrepreneurs are finding new ways to package information into a form people will buy.' *Venture*, 2, 1980.

Jones, Thomas F. *Entrepreneurism: the Mythical, the True, and the New*. New York: Donald I. Fine Inc, 1987.

Josephine, Helen B. 'Intrepreneurship in fee-based information services.' *Journal of Library Administration*, 10 (2/3), 1989.

Judy Macfarlane at the Price Waterhouse Business Information Center: Bringing intrapreneurial services to the Montréal business community,' in *InfoManage: The International Management Newsletter for the Information Services Executive*, 2 (8) July, 1995.

Kanter, Rosabeth Moss. *The Change Masters: Innovation and Entrepreneurship in the American Corporation*. New York: Simon & Schuster, 1983.

Kanter, Rosabeth Moss. 'The new managerial work.' *Harvard Business Review*, November/December, 1989.

Kanter, Rosabeth Moss. *When Giants Learn to Dance*. New York: Simon & Schuster, 1989.

King, Don and José-Marie Griffiths. *Special Libraries and Information Services – Increasing the Information Edge*. Rockville, MD: Information Frontiers Publications.

Kniffel, Leonardo. 'Is it morally correct to be repelled by money?' [Editorial] *American Libraries*, October, 1990.

Kushel, Gerald. *Reaching the Peak Performance Zone: How to Motivate Yourself and Others to Excel*. New York: American Management Association, 1994.

Landau, Ralph. 'Corporate partnering can spur innovation.' *Research Management*, May/June, 1987, p. 22.

Lau, Theresa and K.F. Chan. 'The incident method: an alternative way of studying entrepreneurial behavior.' *Irish Business and Administrative Research*, 15, 1994.

Levitt, Theodore. 'Marketing intangible products and product intangibles.' *Harvard Business Review*, May/June, 1987.

'Mark Merrifield's entrepreneurial approach to public librarianship.' *InfoManage: The International Management Newsletter for the Information Services Executive*, 2 (1), December, 1994.

Marshall, Edward M. *Transforming the Work We Do: the Power of the Collaborative Workplace*. New York: American Management Association, 1995.

Mason, Florence M. 'Libraries, entrepreneurship, and risk.' *Journal of Library Administration*, 10 (2/3), 1989.

Matarazzo, James M. *Corporate Library Excellence*. Washington DC: Special Libraries Association, 1990.

Matarazzo, James M. and Miriam A. Drake. *Information for Management: A Handbook*. Washington DC: Special Libraries Association, 1994.

McClelland, D.C. 'Characteristics of successful entrepreneurs.' *Journal of Creative Behavior*, 21 (3), 1986.

Megill, Kenneth A. *Making the Information Revolution: A Handbook on Federal Information Resources Management*. Silver Spring, MD: Association for Information and Image Management, 1995.

Monty, Vivienne. 'Why don't you get your priorities straight?' *The SpeciaList* (Washington DC: Special Libraries Association), 16 (6), June, 1993.

Mount, Ellis. *Special Libraries and Information Centers*. Washington DC: Special Libraries Association, 1995.

Nathan, John. *Inc*, 11 (4), April, 1989.

'OPLs in Germany move to enhance status; formal steps taken to structure one-person librarianship as 'a distinct discipline' in information services.' *The One-Person Library: A Newsletter for Librarians and Management*, 12 (2), June, 1995.

Orna, Elizabeth. *Practical Information Policies: How to Manage Information Flow in Organizations*. Brookfield, VT: Gower, 1990.

Orna, Elizabeth. 'Why you need an information policy – and how to sell it.' *Aslib Information*, 21 (5), May, 1993.

Osterman, Paul. 'The impact of IT on jobs and skills.' *The Corporation of the 1990s: Information Technology and Organizational Transformation*. Michael S. Scott Morton, ed. New York: Oxford University Press, 1991.

Parker, Sara. 'Innovation in state libraries.' *Journal of Library Administration*, 10 (2/3), 1989.

Penniman, David R. 'Shaping the future: the Council on Library Resources helps to fund change.' *Library Journal*, 117 (17), October 15, 1992.

Peters, Paul Evan. 'Information age avatars.' *Library Journal*, 120, (5), March 15, 1995.

Peters, Tom. *The Tom Peters Seminar: Crazy Tim.*

Piggott, Sylvia. 'Why corporate librarians must reengineer the library for the new information age.' *Special Libraries*, 86 (1), Winter, 1995.

Pinchot, Gifford III. *Intrapreneuring: Why You Don't Have to Leave the Corporation to Become an Entrepreneur*, New York: Harper & Row, 1985.

Pinchot, Gifford III. 'Innovation through intrapreneurship.' *Research Management*, March/April, 1987.

Powell, Alan. 'Management models and measurement in the virtual library.' *Special Libraries*, 85 (4), Fall, 1994.

Prusak, Laurence. 'Corporate librarians: a soft analysis, a warning, some generic advice.' in Matarazzo, James M. and Miriam A. Drake, eds. *Information for Management: A Handbook*. Washington DC: Special Libraries Association, 1994.

Radar, Hannelore B. 'Teamwork and Entrepreneurship.' *Journal of Library Administration*, 10 (2/3), 1989.

Reilly, Barnard J. and Joseph A. DiAngelo. 'Entrepreneurial behavior in large organizations.' *SAM Advanced Management Journal*, Summer, 1987.

Riggs, Donald E. 'Entrepreneurial spirit in strategic planning.' *Journal of Library Administration*, 8 (1), Spring, 1987.

Riggs, Donald E. 'Making creative, innovative, and entrepreneurial things happen in the special library.' *Journal of Library Administration*, 10 (2/3), 1989.

Ross, J.E. 'Intrapreneurship and corporate culture.' *Industrial Management*, 29 (1), January–February, 1987.

Ruben, B.D. 'The coming information age: information, technology, and the study of behavior,' in B.D. Ruben, ed. *Information and Behavior*, Vol. 1. New Brunswick, NJ: Transaction, 1985.

Shane, Scott A. 'Are champions different from non-champions?' *Journal of Business Venturing*, 9 (5), September, 1994.

Sheehy, Gail. *Pathfinders*. New York: William Morrow and Company, 1981.

'SLA's solo librarians now online: solos' Internet listserv a smashing success.' *The One-Person Library: A Newsletter for Librarians and Management*, 12 (4), August, 1995.

Souder, William E. 'Stimulating and managing ideas.' *Research Management*, 30 (3), May/June, 1987.

St. Clair, Guy. *Power and Influence: Enhancing Information Services Within the Organization*. London and New Brunswick, NJ: Bowker-Saur, 1994.

St. Clair, Guy. *Customer Service in the Information Environment*. London and New Brunswick, NJ: Bowker-Saur, 1994.

Stahl, Gail. 'Fees for library and information services: strategic and practical considerations.' *Library Management Quarterly*, 14 (3), Spring, 1991.

Stevenson, Howard H. and J. Carlos Jarillo. 'A paradigm of entrepreneurship: entrepreneurial management.' *Strategic Management Journal*, 11, 1990.

Stopford, John M. and Charles W.F. Baden-Fuller. 'Creating corporate entrepreneurship.' *Strategic Management Journal*. 15 (7), September, 1994.

'Sylvia Piggott at the Bank of Montréal: Reengineering information services for the 2nd era of the information age.' *InfoManage: The International Management Newsletter for the Information Services Executive*, 2 (3), February, 1995.

Szilagyi, Andrew D. Jr. *Management and Performance*. New York: Scott, Foresman, 1988.

Thornton, Paul B. 'The seeds of positive growth.' *Personal Selling Power*, November/December, 1994.

Veaner, Allen B. 'Introduction' *President's Task Force on the Value of the Information Professional – Final Report, Preliminary Study*. Washington DC: Special Libraries Association, 1987.

Wallace, Danny P. and Kathleen M. Heim. 'Creativity in library and information science education: implications for curriculum design.' *Journal of Library Administration*, 10 (2/3), 1989.

Warner, Alice Sizer. 'Librarians as money makers: the bottom line.' *American Libraries*, November, 1990.

Webb, T. D. and Edward A. Jensen. 'Managing innovative information technology.' *Journal of Library Administration*, 10 (2/3), 1989.

Weinstein, Lois. 'LIFENET/INTERNET and the health science librarian.' *Special Libraries*, 85 (1), Winter, 1994.

Weitzen, H.S. 'Infopreneurs: turn data into dollars.' *Information Management Review*, 5 (1), 1989.

Weitzen, H.S. *Infopreneurs: Turning Data Into Dollars*. New York: Wiley, 1988.

White, Herbert S. 'Entrepreneurship and the library profession.' *Journal of Library Administration*, 8 (1), Spring, 1987.

Woodsworth, Anne and James F. Williams II. *Managing the Economics of Owning, Leasing and Contracting Out Information Services*. Brookfield, VT: Ashgate, 1993.

Index